Pinterest Marketing

by Christine Martinez and Barbara Boyd

ALPHA

A member of Penguin Group (USA) Inc.

ALPHA BOOKS

Published by Penguin Group (USA) Inc.

Penguin Group (USA) Inc., 375 Hudson Street, New York, New York 10014, USA • Penguin Group (Canada), 90 Eglinton Avenue East, Suite 700, Toronto, Ontario M4P 2Y3, Canada (a division of Pearson Penguin Canada Inc.) • Penguin Books Ltd., 80 Strand, London WC2R 0RL, England • Penguin Ireland, 25 St. Stephen's Green, Dublin 2, Ireland (a division of Penguin Books Ltd.) • Penguin Group (Australia), 250 Camberwell Road, Camberwell, Victoria 3124, Australia (a division of Pearson Australia Group Pty. Ltd.) • Penguin Books India Pvt. Ltd., 11 Community Centre, Panchsheel Park, New Delhi—110 017, India • Penguin Group (NZ), 67 Apollo Drive, Rosedale, North Shore, Auckland 1311, New Zealand (a division of Pearson New Zealand Ltd.) • Penguin Books (South Africa) (Pty.) Ltd., 24 Sturdee Avenue, Rosebank, Johannesburg 2196, South Africa • Penguin Books Ltd., Registered Offices: 80 Strand, London WC2R 0RL, England

International Standard Book Number: 978-1-61564-234-2
Library of Congress Catalog Card Number: 2012939814

14 13 12   8 7 6 5 4 3 2 1

Interpretation of the printing code: The rightmost number of the first series of numbers is the year of the book's printing; the rightmost number of the second series of numbers is the number of the book's printing. For example, a printing code of 12-1 shows that the first printing occurred in 2012.

Printed in the United States of America

Note: This publication contains the opinions and ideas of its authors. It is intended to provide helpful and informative material on the subject matter covered. It is sold with the understanding that the authors and publisher are not engaged in rendering professional services in the book. If the reader requires personal assistance or advice, a competent professional should be consulted.

The authors and publisher specifically disclaim any responsibility for any liability, loss, or risk, personal or otherwise, which is incurred as a consequence, directly or indirectly, of the use and application of any of the contents of this book.

Most Alpha books are available at special quantity discounts for bulk purchases for sales promotions, premiums, fund-raising, or educational use. Special books, or book excerpts, can also be created to fit specific needs. For details, write: Special Markets, Alpha Books, 375 Hudson Street, New York, NY 10014.

Publisher: *Mike Sanders*

Executive Managing Editor: *Billy Fields*

Executive Acquisitions Editor: *Lori Cates Hand*

Senior Development Editor: *Christy Wagner*

Senior Production Editor: *Kayla Dugger*

Copy Editor: *Amy Borrelli*

Cover Designer: *Rebecca Batchelor*

Book Designers: *William Thomas, Rebecca Batchelor*

Indexer: *Brad Herriman*

Layout: *Ayanna Lacey*

Proofreader: *John Etchison*

Contents

Appendixes

Introduction

The faster and better technology works—think download times and screen quality—the more we come to rely on images instead of words to make an impact and to make quick judgments and decisions. Images have a personal, intuitive effect. Decisions are made before your mind has time to think about something. Pinterest's success has everything to do with the immediacy of relating to an image and sharing it with the world. You see something, you like it, you want it, or you want to show it to someone. It's about a nonintrusive personal connection, finding other people who share your interests but don't want to know all your secrets.

The nonintrusive yet personal factor makes Pinterest the perfect platform for business. Businesses today have to build and maintain relationships. It's about knowing what your customers and clients like, understanding their needs, and fulfilling them. At the same time, your clients don't necessarily want to be your *friends*. It's a mutually beneficial relationship: the business helps the customer obtain or do X in her life, and the customer helps the business by buying the service or product. It's about collaborating.

Without a doubt, Pinterest has to be a part of your online marketing strategy, right up there next to Facebook and Twitter. You reach a different audience with each social media platform, and adding Pinterest to your branding and marketing strategy expands your reach. We're here to show you how to do it.

What's in This Book

We divided this book into tasks, strategies, and tactics. Keep in mind, we'd love for you to read the book cover to cover (and even let us know what you think), but the truth is, you can read only the parts that apply most to you. If you're a strong marketing strategist but know nothing about using Pinterest, you want to begin with Part 1, and just with that information, we're sure the ideas of how to fit Pinterest into your marketing strategy will begin to flow. If you're a Pinterest expert already but don't know a lot about promoting your business, you probably don't need to read Part 1, but Parts 2 and 3 are essential for you to get the most out of Pinterest, and this book.

Here's how each part breaks down:

Pinterest is a straightforward, easy-to-use social media platform. In **Part 1, Getting Started with Pinterest,** we explain the philosophy behind Pinterest and why it makes a great marketing tool for most businesses. That philosophy is something you should keep in mind while reading the rest of the book and applying the tools we provide. In these chapters, we take you through the steps of setting up your account, highlight the Pinterest lingo (like *pins* and *boards*), and show you how to use the tools Pinterest provides for pinning.

If you're intrigued by marketing and want to take your business to a new level, **Part 2, Pinning Down Your Marketing Strategy,** leads you through the steps to do just that. We ask you specific questions to help you identify where you want your business to go and discover how Pinterest can help you get there. Going back to the Pinterest philosophy, we explain how to tell your brand or business story through images and create a narrative that inspires present customers to bring more business your way and leads future customers to your doorstep. After you define your strategy—the conceptual idea of how you're going to meet your business goals—you're ready for Part 3.

Part 3, Implementing Your Pinterest Tactics, gets into the nitty-gritty of applying the specific Pinterest tasks that support your strategy and bring you closer to your business goal. Pinterest isn't a stand-alone tactic, however, so we explore ways of integrating Pinterest with other online marketing efforts such as your website, blog, and presence on other social media sites. When you finish reading Part 3, you'll have concrete tasks to put into practice.

Like a garden or a child, you can't just create a Pinterest presence and then leave, expecting it to grow by itself. You have to curate and maintain it. Some businesses sign on to Pinterest, build a few boards, and leave after a month, claiming it's a waste of time. Our experience is that, just like Pinterest built slowly to blockbuster status, it takes time, consistency, and perseverance to see the effect Pinterest is having on your success. In **Part 4, Taking Pinterest Further,** we explain how to measure the initial and ongoing impact and effectiveness of your efforts, and we also give you clear instructions for maintaining and growing your Pinterest presence.

At the end of the book we share a glossary of terms you should know, along with resources to carry you along on your Pinterest journey.

Extras

Throughout the book, we've scattered extra bits of information in sidebars. Here's what to look for:

DEFINITION

These sidebars define Pinterest and marketing terms you may not be familiar with.

MARKETING MIX-UP

Heed these warnings to avoid Pinterest and marketing snafus.

PIN TIP

Here you find tips and tricks that enhance your Pinterest marketing efforts.

VERY PINTERESTING!

Look here for fun facts that add sparkle to your marketing or dinner party conversations.

Acknowledgments

Barbara would like to thank Christine for her energy and pinthusiasm, and Carole Jelen and Zack Romano at Waterside Productions for inviting her to collaborate on this project. Most of all, Barbara thanks her husband, Ugo de Paula, for his love, patience, and ongoing support of all her endeavors, writing and otherwise.

Special Thanks to the Technical Reviewer

The Complete Idiot's Guide to Pinterest Marketing was reviewed by an expert who double-checked the accuracy of what you'll learn here, to help us ensure that this book gives you everything you need to know about boosting your brand's image on Pinterest. Special thanks are extended to Annalise Kaylor.

Annalise is director of social media marketing at Intrapromote (intrapromote.com), a boutique social media marketing and search engine optimization agency. Over the last decade, she has helped brands establish their social media strategy, lent her social media expertise to sites like Mashable.com and ReadWriteWeb.com, and served as a panelist for industry conferences such as South by Southwest Interactive.

Trademarks

All terms mentioned in this book that are known to be or are suspected of being trademarks or service marks have been appropriately capitalized. Alpha Books and Penguin Group (USA) Inc. cannot attest to the accuracy of this information. Use of a term in this book should not be regarded as affecting the validity of any trademark or service mark.

Getting Started with Pinterest

If you're familiar with how Pinterest works, you know how easy Pinterest is to use, and we won't be offended if you skip Part 1. If, on the other hand, your manager gave you this book and said, "You're in charge of our Pinterest presence" but you have only a faint inkling about what Pinterest is, read on.

Chapter 1 fills you in on why so many people love Pinterest and how your business can benefit from including Pinterest as part of your online marketing efforts. Chapter 2 delves into the technical aspects of creating an account and gives you some pointers—from a marketing standpoint—for making the most of the information on your profile. In Chapters 3 and 4, we explain the practical side of creating boards and pinning images, as well as other types of media, on those boards. Throughout these step-by-step chapters, we indicate the type of impact each task has on your overall marketing plan.

What Is Pinterest?

In This Chapter

- Social media with a photo focus
- Understanding Pinterest's popularity
- The best brands for Pinterest
- A look at Pinterest's user base
- The power of Pinterest for brands

Pinterest (pronounced *PIN-ter-est*) is the latest and greatest social media sensation to hit the web. Pinterest is a virtual pinboard, or virtual bulletin board of sorts, that allows you to share the interesting, beautiful, and inspiring things you find on the web, and organize them into categorized pinboards you create for yourself. Because Pinterest is an open social platform, you can also browse boards created by other users to discover new things and gather inspiration from friends and family, brands you love, and users who share your interests. According to Pinterest, the main idea behind the site is to "connect everyone in the world through the 'things' they find interesting."

Pinterest users utilize the site for a variety of different reasons. Some are cultivators of content and enjoy the process of sourcing and sharing the most exciting products and images on the web. Others simply enjoy browsing the site to gather information and inspiration by "repinning" from other users' boards. Other popular uses of Pinterest include gathering favorite recipes, planning weddings, decorating homes, and finding inspiration and instructions for DIY and craft projects. That's a lot for a single site!

The Visual Social Media Site

Pinterest is a social networking site based on sharing images. We like to think of it as a cross between Tumblr and Flickr. While a social networking site like Facebook can also be very visual, Pinterest is entirely image driven. It does not allow for standalone messages of any kind without an image first placed on the site. Although it's important to include a thoughtful description of the images you share on Pinterest (something we discuss in detail later in the book), sharing beautiful images on Pinterest is the site's top priority and primary function.

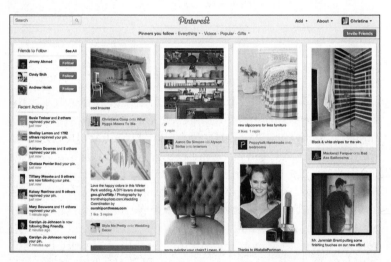

One glance at Pinterest's home page and you can see how visual the site is.

With its visual focus and enormous initial impact on the web, it's clear that Pinterest represents the next generation of socially networked communication that's moving in a less words/more photos direction.

This visual trend has been a long time coming. It started as brands and power users on Facebook began to notice that when they shared images, engagement with users increased in a major way. Social sites like Tumblr and Instagram have also capitalized on this visual trend. Tumblr allows its users to *micro-blog* with the emphasis on sharing images. This type of fast and easy image-focused blogging enables those who blog through Tumblr the opportunity to post several times a day.

DEFINITION

Micro-blogging is the act of posting very short entries or updates on a blog or social networking site.

This Tumblr blog format clearly favors images over text.

With Instagram, users can snap images with their smartphones and share them with their network of followers. Instagram enables users to comment on posted photographs, which encourages conversations around the images published. Instagram's surging popularity and enthusiastic fan base is yet another prime example of the push toward the explosive visual trend on the internet.

A view of the popular social application Instagram as seen through the website Webstagram.

Visual social networking sites like Tumblr and Instagram have had a lot of success over the past couple years, but neither has seen the kind of skyrocketing growth Pinterest has since its launch in March 2010. Pinterest has quickly become *the* visual social media site and has solidified a new age in which we are experiencing the web as a more dynamic visual medium.

The Fastest-Growing Site in History

Pinterest's primarily visual nature has resonated with its early users in such a way that many of these users would describe the site as "addictive." Both *pin addicts* and new users who join the site daily fall in love with the visceral experience they have on Pinterest. This type of emotionally engaging experience, in combination with the site's ease of use, are two major components that have contributed to Pinterest becoming the fastest-growing site in history.

DEFINITION

A **pin addict** is a Pinterest user who would consider himself or herself an advocate of the site. This person also spends a considerable amount of time using Pinterest.

In January 2012, comScore reported the site had 11.7 million unique users, making it the fastest site in history to break through the 10 million unique-visitor mark. This was an amazing and unprecedented feat by Pinterest, the visual new kid on the block.

While many social media skeptics would argue that Pinterest is yet another social media craze whose popularity will surely fizzle out and give way to the next, a ton of compelling evidence shows Pinterest is here to stay for the foreseeable future. Based on a study published by Shareaholic in January 2012, Pinterest drove more referral traffic to sites in January than Google+, Reddit, YouTube, LinkedIn, and MySpace combined!

Several key components contribute to Pinterest's success. In an article titled "A Scrapbook on the Web Catches Fire," published in *The New York Times* in February 2012, tech columnist David Pogue explains why he believes there's plenty of room in the social media spotlight for a site like Pinterest:

- Pinterest is clean: "It's pure, uncluttered and non-blinky. There are no ads, scrolling columns or pop-up anything."
- Pinterest is personal: Unlike Facebook and Twitter, Pinterest is "not just broadcasting, or even principally broadcasting. You create Pinterest boards for your own use, your own memory-jogging, your own inspiration."
- Pinterest is humble: It "gives you a break from the usual goal of social sites: self-absorption, self-documenting and self-promotion."

This third point Pogue makes is one that really sets Pinterest apart from other major social media sites and seems to truly resonate with those who have fallen in love with the site.

People want to be able to engage with others on a personal level. Until Pinterest, social interaction on the web had taken on a superficial tone. In *The Times* article, Pogue goes on to point out a recent Huffington Post entry that stated, "Facebook and Twitter posts tend to come with the silent subtext, 'Here's how great I am.' On Pinterest, the tone seems to be 'Wouldn't this be great?'"

Being able to connect with others around personal interests creates a genuine experience, and a genuine experience has been nearly impossible to capture on the web until now. It's no wonder millions of users spend hours a day on Pinterest and why Pinterest has become the fastest-growing site in history.

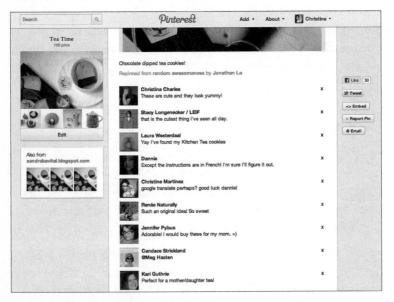

This photo shows an engaging Pinterest conversation based around a common interest—chocolate-dipped tea cookies!

Brands That Thrive on Pinterest

With Pinterest's visual nature, it seems pretty obvious that some brands have a greater advantage on this social media platform than others. The current U.S. Pinterest demographic also makes it a more advantageous platform for many female-focused brands, but we discuss that further in the next section. For now, let's spend some time focusing on which brands are a perfect fit for Pinterest, and which have to get especially creative to make this platform work for them.

> **PIN TIP**
>
> Keep in mind that while Pinterest is better suited for some brands over others, just about any brand can and should find a use for this hot new social media platform. Read on for useful tips on how to make Pinterest work for your brand!

Brands that have a great deal of visual content around what they do, be it products or services, have a much easier time figuring out how to market themselves on Pinterest. Generally, when brands get started on Pinterest, the natural inclination is to feed the site visual content from their website or blog. Therefore, if a brand has a lot of visual content to share, getting started on Pinterest feels a lot more natural, and these brands are likely to "pin on," or continue to add their content to the site.

Take, for example, a brand like the Travel Channel. Pinterest is a brilliant social media fit for it, because of how visual the experience of traveling is. The Travel Channel covers a wide range of travel-related and global topics across hundreds of television programs. Just about all the Travel Channel's communication is done visually, making Pinterest a wonderful place for it to pin onto a range of visually stunning and compelling boards its favorite still shots, photographs from around the world, travel inspiration for the adventurous, and beautiful and unique cultures that cover our globe.

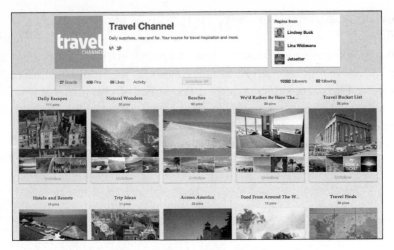

The Travel Channel's Pinterest page contains a nice collection of inspiring boards.

As mentioned earlier in this section, brands that are able to cater to Pinterest's overwhelmingly female audience also have a lot of success marketing on Pinterest. At the moment, wedding-industry brands like *Martha Stewart Weddings* magazine are doing very well visually communicating and marketing themselves on Pinterest.

Martha Stewart Weddings *magazine has a strong grasp on how to create board after board of beautiful content.*

Martha Stewart Weddings magazine is the type of brand made for Pinterest. Not only does it have endless amounts of gorgeous images to share and inspire Pinterest users, it's also able to capture the prime demographic currently on the site. We like to think of brands like this as having the Pinterest perfect storm: archives of bright and beautiful imagery, tons of interesting content around a major industry, and extremely female-friendly subject matter.

Pinterest perfect storm brands thrive on Pinterest. However—and we can't stress this enough—this doesn't mean your brand can't have a tremendous amount of success on Pinterest as well. Throughout this book, we highlight plenty of brands that are rocking the Pinterest world—including some you might be surprised about. From super-market chains to yogurt companies, most brands are finding their place on Pinterest with a lot of thought and creativity.

DEFINITION

A **Pinterest perfect storm brand** is a brand ideally suited for Pinterest because of the visual content it produces and the demographic it targets.

Getting to Know the Pinterest Demographic

Knowing and understanding the demographics on Pinterest is a great place to start when you're in the process of figuring out how to use this site to market your brand. There are key pieces of information you're going to want to pay attention to when planning your company's social media plan on Pinterest. Luckily, the talented folks at Modea, a digital ad agency in Virginia, created an easy-to-understand infographic explaining Pinterest's user base. This infographic was based on information sourced from comScore and Tech Crunch.

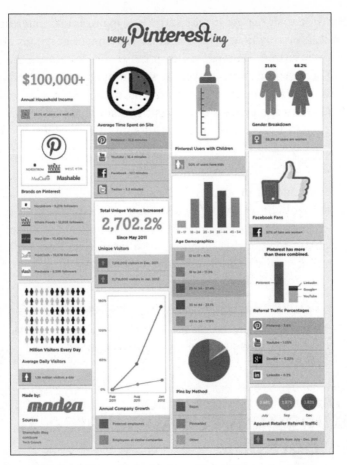

This fun infographic by Modea explains Pinterest's user demographic.

The gender breakdown is the first bit of information that's important to note. As of March 2012, 68.2 percent of Pinterest users were women. While Pinterest is starting to gain in popularity with men (early on, it was reported that as many as 98 percent of users were women), the site is still heavily dominated by female users. This means brands like yours that are starting to develop a presence on Pinterest are better off pinning content that resonates with a female audience.

With regard to age demographics, the vast majority of Pinterest users fall between the ages of 25 and 44. This piece of data is also incredibly important because it's essential that brands target their Pinterest campaign efforts to appeal to this age group. For instance, Nordstrom carries a large selection of apparel and accessories from a wide range of age groups. However, the majority of Nordstrom's Pinterest boards and pins are targeted for the 25-to-44 age group. Nordstrom was also mindful of Pinterest's gender breakdown. Only 1 of their 30 boards is targeted toward men.

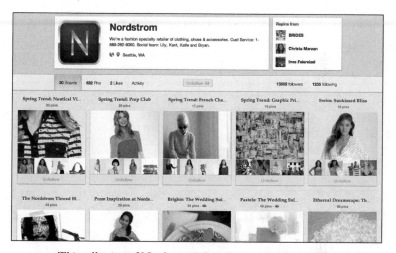

This collection of Nordstrom's boards are geared toward women.

Why Should I Use Pinterest to Market My Business?

Looking back at all the information on the Modea infographic, it's clear why brands are starting to jump on and market through Pinterest. Pinterest is driving incredible amounts of traffic to retail sites and businesses. For example, apparel retailer referral traffic from Pinterest rose 289 percent between July and December 2011.

It's important to note that Pinterest isn't just driving traffic; recent data beginning to emerge is showing that Pinterest is also driving sales. Take, for example, the article published by Mashable in April 2012 titled "Pinterest Becomes Sales Driver for Major Home Goods Store." In it, Wayfair CEO Niraj Shah reported that shoppers coming to his company's website from Pinterest are 10 percent more likely to make a purchase and will spend 10 percent more than those referred to Wayfair from Facebook or Twitter. When asked why he thinks Pinterest has been a stronger sales channel than other social media platforms, Shah explained, "Pinterest encourages people to collect images that inspire them, and that includes products. Visual imagery drives inspiration, it's what makes you want to buy it. We sell things [on our sites] in the same way."

Wayfair's boards showcase their wide selection of products.

The potential for referral traffic sales is huge on Pinterest, as evident by the early statistics starting to emerge. And it's really just the beginning. As of March 2012, Pinterest had an incredible 2.2 million active daily users and approximately 12 million active users every month. With numbers like these climbing at a rapid rate, Pinterest has solidified itself as the newest social media must for brands all over the world.

But if for some reason the statistics on Pinterest alone haven't convinced you, there's another major reason why your brand should be preparing to jump on board: Pinterest is an incredible source of information about your customers and clients. And not only is it important to understand the behaviors and interests of your target customers, it's equally important to gather information about how they interact with your brand. This is an excellent way to gauge what your brand is doing well and what still needs to be improved.

Pinterest users are constantly searching for products they would love for themselves, and products they'd love to recommend to other users. According to an infographic created by *PC Magazine*, Pinterest users are essentially acting as "word-of-mouth marketing teams that are directing buyers, doers, and seekers to your online and mobile properties." This type of word-of-mouth marketing is incredibly successful at creating brand awareness for otherwise unknown and small label brands.

This clever infographic by PC Magazine *illustrates how Pinterest users are spreading the word about brands and products.*

If nothing else, Pinterest can act as a free focus group for your brand, providing you with useful information on how to create a stronger web presence and improve sales every day.

Convinced? Great! Now let's get you started with everything you need to know about marketing on Pinterest.

The Least You Need to Know

- Pinterest is a virtual pinboard that enables you to share the interesting, beautiful, and inspiring things you find online.
- Unlike Facebook and Twitter, Pinterest is almost entirely visual, and most of the communication is via photographs and images.
- Because of its visual nature, users are able to get emotionally engaged with Pinterest and are spending a considerable amount of time on the site.
- Brands that have a great deal of visual content to share can have a lot of success using Pinterest as a social marketing platform.
- Pinterest is not only driving massive amounts of traffic to retailers; a considerable amount of sales are also being generated by user recommendations on the site.
- Pinterest is a great place to learn about the likes, dislikes, and behaviors of your target customer.

Pinterest
First Steps

In This Chapter

- Signing up for a Pinterest account
- Establishing your Pinterest identity
- Installing the Pin It bookmarklet
- Modifying your profile preferences

Getting started with Pinterest is easy, as you'll learn in this chapter. It almost takes longer to read the instructions than to actually complete the process!

In this chapter, we take you step-by-step through the account setup process and give you tips for choosing an effective Pinterest account name—one that will help your existing and potential customers find you. We explain how to install the Pin It bookmarklet on the bookmarks or favorites bar of your web browser so you can pin images directly from the website where you find them. We also go over the profile preferences so you can customize your profile to best market yourself or your business on Pinterest.

Remember, everything you do on Pinterest helps create a cohesive brand identity, so as you go through each step of the process, make decisions based on the message you want to send to your customers.

No Invitation Needed

For the first couple years of its existence, Pinterest allowed users to join only if they were invited by other users. The invitation-only policy was promotional genius in the style of multilevel marketing or chain letters: you tell two friends, and they tell two friends, and so on, and so on.

Think about it. Are you more trusting of a company that says "Join us!" or a friend who says "Look what I'm doing! Come with me!"? By joining Pinterest, you benefit from its marketing genius by using *your customers* to tell others about your products and services.

But in August 2012, Pinterest opened up for anyone to join without an invitation. The official announcement alluded to the fact that Pinterest finally had the capacity to handle more people.

You can (and later we tell you why you should) still invite people to join Pinterest, but you don't have to worry about being parsimonious with your invitation allotment.

Pinterest accounts no longer have to be tied to Facebook or Twitter. As a business, you want to link your social media accounts to create cross-marketing opportunities; but individuals who opt not to use Facebook or Twitter are no longer excluded from the Pinterest fun—and that's good news for you, as it broadens your potential client base.

The sign-up screen.

Creating Your Pinterest Identity

Regardless of how you receive an invitation, to set up your account, you're asked to use your Facebook or Twitter username or your email address and password. (We assume your business has one or all of these.) Pinterest looks at your Facebook and Twitter friends to see who you know who already uses Pinterest. Remember, Pinterest is all about sharing with who you know and who they know, and following and being followed; your existing community is the best place to begin your marketing efforts!

Here's how to create your account: go to pinterest.com and click the **Join Pinterest** button. Sign up with either your Facebook or Twitter account or your email address.

Use your business-specific username or email and password so Pinterest links with that account, not your personal account. If you want to set up a personal Pinterest account, the procedure is the same, but we're talking business here.

To sign up using your Facebook account, click the **Sign-Up With Facebook** button, and type in your Facebook username or email and password. The Facebook app screen opens on your Facebook News Feed.

MARKETING MIX-UP

You have to use a Facebook account, not a Facebook page, to set up your Pinterest account.

Choose the level of Pinterest activity you want revealed on Facebook from the **Friends** pop-up menu in the lower left of the dialog box. We suggest you choose **Public**. Click the **Go To App** button.

To sign up with Twitter, click on **Twitter** next to the Facebook button. Type in your Twitter username and password, and click **Sign In**. Because you must use a Facebook account, not a Facebook page, Twitter may be a better option for you. Click your email address to create an account independent of Facebook or Twitter. You can link either to your account at any time after your account is created. You can unlink your account after it's created by editing your Pinterest settings, as explained in Facebook and Twitter Options under the "Personalizing Your Profile Settings" section later in this chapter.

If you used Facebook or Twitter, a Create Account screen appears. Pinterest takes your profile image from whichever social media you chose. (We explain how to change this image in the "Personalizing Your Profile Settings" section later in this chapter.) The fields are blank if you use your email address to create an account. You can upload a photo by clicking **Upload Your Photo** and then scrolling through the directories and files to find an image. Click the image you want, then click **Choose**. If you don't choose to upload a photo at this point, you can do it later; in the meantime, a pushpin icon will be displayed next to your name.

Type in your desired username—probably your business name—in the **Username** field. If you choose a username that's already in use, a message appears below the field that reads **The username is already in use.** Keep trying until this is replaced with "no message appears."

PIN TIP

Choose a username that's easy to remember and links to you so your customers and followers can find you easily. If your blog or website has a catchy name, like MilesToStyle, use that to reinforce brand identity and awareness. If you're most known by your name, use that or a variation of it. If you have multiple brands, you can create multiple Pinterest identities, or one identity and multiple boards. (We explore the pros and cons of each scenario in Chapter 8.)

Type in the email address you want to associate with this Pinterest account. Again, this should be a business email address. It doesn't have to be the same email you use for Twitter or Facebook. You may even want to use a different email address for your Pinterest activity.

Type a password you want to associate with your Pinterest account. For security reasons, you should use a unique password, not the one that goes with the email address. Choose a password that's easy for you to remember but hard for others to guess. Pinterest requires you to use a password of at least six alphanumeric characters.

VERY PINTERESTING!

The longer and more complex your password, the less likely it will be hacked.

After you type the required information in the fields and upload your photo, click **Create Account**.

The next screen displays images and asks that you choose five to get started with your pins. This lets Pinterest know what you're interested in. After you choose five images, the **Continue** button appears at the bottom. Click it and Pinterest opens to the Pinterest home page.

In the meantime a message arrives in your email inbox asking you to verify your email address. Go to your email and click the **Verify** button. You will return to your Pinterest home page, ready to begin pinning or to change your settings.

Create your Pinterest account.

You are now the newest Pinterest member. Welcome to the club!

Completing the Account Setup

Your account is now set up, but there are three tasks that help the Pinterest identity you created grow: selecting who you want to follow, creating your boards, and adding the Pin It bookmarklet to your web browser.

Finding and Following Your Interests

Following your brand-related interests on Pinterest is important. After all, you want to surround yourself with like-minded pinners who are likely your target audience and potential customers. We dive into this topic more in Chapter 13, but for now, let's see how it works.

After you click the **Create Account** button, the next screen shows a selection of thumbnail images. When you select images you like, Pinterest begins to form an idea about which categories and pinners might interest you. Pinterest will choose pinners for you to follow based on the images you choose. Click your name in the upper-right corner to open your profile. You see the pinners Pinterest chose for you to follow and you see your empty boards.

You can unfollow any or all of these automatically selected boards at any time by clicking the **Unfollow** button below the pinboard's thumbnail image. You may want to unfollow boards that contain pins that don't mesh well with your brand identity. You can also choose to unfollow a person completely by opening their profile and clicking **Unfollow All**. The pinners Pinterest gives you to follow aren't always ones you would choose, and this is a way to stop following a pinner completely.

To add people you know already, such as Facebook friends, click your name to open the pop-up menu and choose **Find Friends**. In the screen that appears, click one of the tabs—Facebook, Gmail, or Yahoo!—and Pinterest will match up people you know from that source with people who are on Pinterest. Two lists appear: one lists your Facebook friends who aren't on Pinterest; an Invite button next to each name gives you the opportunity to send Pinterest invitations. The other lists your Facebook friends who have Pinterest accounts, and clicking the **Follow** button next to each name adds that person to the people you follow. You can also click **Follow All** to quickly increase who you follow. When you follow someone, you see their pins on the Pinterest home screen when you log in.

If you want to invite people to Pinterest, click the **Email** tab and type in your friends' email addresses, add a brief note, and click **Send Invites**.

Creating Your First Boards

Now the fun begins—you're ready to create some of your own boards! We go in depth on using your boards as a marketing and branding tool in Chapter 8, but stick with us here as we explain the basics of creating your first boards.

When you click your name in the upper-right corner, your profile shows that you have no boards. Click the **Board Name** field and type a title for the board you want to create. Repeat on the other blank boards.

Now the fun begins—you're ready to create some of your own boards! We go in depth on using your boards as a marketing and branding tool in Chapter 8, but stick with us here as we explain the basics of creating your first boards.

Here's how to create boards: click the **Create Boards** button at the top or bottom of the window. The **Create Your First Pinboards** screen appears.

Pinterest helps you get started by suggesting pinboard titles.

You can add, delete, or rearrange the order of your boards, as well as invite other people to contribute to your boards. We explain all this and more about boards in Chapter 3.

Adding the Pin It Bookmarklet to Your Web Browser

Pinterest has a tool that helps you quickly and easily pin images you find on the web: adding a bookmarklet, which Pinterest also calls the "Pin It button," or "pinmarklet," to the bookmarks bar or favorites of your web browser. (We use the term *bookmarklet* to avoid confusion with the Pin It button you can install on your website or blog.)

Click **About** and choose Pin It Button from the pop-up menu. Pinterest detects which web browser you use and displays the appropriate instructions for adding the Pin It bookmarklet.

Add the Pin It bookmarklet to the bookmarks bar in your web browser.

This bookmarklet, or button, makes pinning a breeze. When you see something you want to pin from a website to one of your boards, click the button to see a selection of all the images on the page. Hover the cursor over the image you want to pin, and click **Pin This** on that image. And then select the board you want to pin it to.

PIN TIP

If you're an iPhone, iPad, or Android user, you can snap a photo of something you see and pin it to one of your boards. We explain using the Pinterest apps in Chapter 4.

Now there's nothing left to do but start pinning! To do this, click **Start Pinning**. In Chapter 10, you learn all about pinning strategically to reinforce brand recognition, increase your customer base, and increase per purchase spending.

Personalizing Your Profile Settings

But wait, there's one thing you might want to do to make your account more complete! That's maximizing your profile settings.

If you're familiar with Facebook, Twitter, and other social media, you realize the importance of your profile settings. Not only do profile settings give you the opportunity to give a bit more (or less) information about yourself or your business, they also control who sees what, and how, about you or your business. Consider the following options to make the most of your profile settings.

To see your profile settings, click **Edit Profile** located above your boards on your profile page. If you're visiting someone else's boards, click the pull-down menu under your name in the upper right of the Pinterest screen, and select **Settings**.

t ▾	Barbara ▾
Invite Friends	
Find Friends	
Boards	
Pins	
Likes	
Settings ▸	
Logout	

*Choose **Settings** from the pull-down menu by your name to personalize your profile settings.*

PIN TIP

As you work through the Edit Profile options, be sure to click **Save Profile**, **Save Settings**, or **Change Password** at the bottom of the relative screen to save your changes.

Editing Your Email Settings

The **Email** field displays the email address you entered at the beginning of your Pinterest account creation. You can change it here if you want Pinterest notifications sent to a different email address.

Click **Change Email Settings** to see a list of notification options. If you turn on an option, you'll receive an email notification when that action occurs. You can also choose how often you receive notifications by clicking the radio button next to **Immediately** or **Once Daily** in the **Frequency** section. Click the **Digest** and **News** radio buttons if you want to receive a weekly activity summary and Pinterest news. Leave them unclicked if you don't. Click **Save Settings** when you finish making your choices.

Changing Your Password

Click **Change Password** to change your password. The screen that appears has three fields: **Old**, **New**, and **New, Again**.

Type your current password in the **Old** field, and type your new password in the **New** and **New, Again** fields. Click **Change Password** at the bottom of the screen to complete the revision.

Language

Click the pop-up menu to select the language you prefer to use on Pinterest.

Editing Your Pinterest Identity

The **First name** and **Last name** fields make up the name that appears above your profile photo when other pinners view your boards. If you used your given name and then decide you want to use your business name or another catchy moniker, you can change it by typing your new choice in **First name** and putting something like "Official" in the **Last name** blank. Pinterest requires you to fill both fields.

Your username is the unique identity associated with your Pinterest account. If at any time you want to change your username, type a new choice in the **Username** field. Remember it has to be a username no one else uses.

As a business, you probably want to leave gender as Unspecified unless you are a one-person show and feel your gender is important to your customers.

Use the **About** field to type a bio about you, your business, or your products. This is the first opportunity you have to add some serious pin appeal to your brand's Pinterest account so be sure you say who you are, what you do, and add something that lends credibility, such as how long you've been in business or the number of Fortune 500 clients you have. You're going to want to pay close attention to Chapter 7 when we discuss writing this information!

We've noticed many companies update or change the **About** field on a regular basis. You can use this field to mention special promotions or to continually reflect your company's evolution.

In the **Location** field, type in your business location or something like universal or world wide web if you have a business that isn't tied to a specific location. If your business is location-based, use your city *and state* or region so people know you're local.

Type in the URL for your business's website in the **Website** field.

Use Pinterest Settings to upload an image and determine how Pinterest interacts with Facebook and Twitter.

Changing Your Visual Image

If you want to use your same profile image from Facebook or Twitter, whichever you used to set up your account, click **Refresh from Facebook** (or **Refresh from Twitter**), and the profile image used there will appear on Pinterest.

If you prefer to use a different image, click **Upload an Image**, and click **Choose File** or **Browse**, depending on which browser you use. A window opens showing the files on your computer. Scroll through the files and directories until you find the image file you want. Click that file and then click **Choose** or **Open**, again, depending on your browser. A thumbnail image replaces the existing image.

> **PIN TIP**
>
> Use your logo as your profile image because it shows up along with your profile name under every image you pin.

Facebook and Twitter Options

You can link Pinterest to your Facebook and Twitter accounts so your Pinterest activity shows up on these other social media outlets.

Click the **Link to Facebook** radio button **ON** to link the two accounts. If you want your Pinterest updates to appear in your Facebook Timeline, click the button next to **Add Pinterest to Facebook Timeline**. Enabling your Pins to appear on Facebook is a great way of letting your existing Facebook community know you're now on Pinterest.

MARKETING MIX-UP

Be sure to click the **Save Profile** button before doing the following **Find Facebook Friends on Pinterest** action because it takes you to a different screen, and you could lose the changes you already made.

To invite Facebook friends to join Pinterest, click **Find Facebook Friends on Pinterest**. A screen appears that presents two lists. The left column shows Facebook friends who aren't on Pinterest. You can invite them one at a time by clicking **Invite** next to each name. A dialog box gives you the option of writing a personalized invitation, after which you click **Send Request** (or **Cancel** if you change your mind). To invite several people at once, click **Invite Friends** at the top of the list. Type your invitation message in the dialog box that appears, and click the radio button next to each friend you want to invite. Click **Send Request** (or **Cancel**) to complete the task.

The right column shows Facebook friends who are also on Pinterest. If you chose to follow those friends when you set up your account, that column will indicate how many Facebook friends you're following. If you chose to follow only some of your Facebook friends, those you aren't yet following appear in the list. Click **Follow** next to each name you want to follow, or click **Follow All** to follow all your outstanding Facebook friends.

As a business, inviting people to join Pinterest can be a tricky thing. Some customers may find it offensive, whereas others may truly want to see what you're up to. It depends on your business and your clientele. Receiving an invitation from JC Penney is different from receiving one from Yoley's Yarns.

On the one hand, people who follow and friend you on Facebook are interested in what you do; on the other hand, it can be perceived as pushy. If you decide inviting Facebook friends to Pinterest is appropriate for your business, a carefully crafted message that accompanies the invitation is essential. This message should let your customers know you appreciate their business and think they would enjoy being a part of Pinterest. A more subtle approach is to add the "Follow Me" button to your website and blog, and post your Pinterest pins on your Facebook timeline. We discuss both tactics in Chapter 10.

We discuss using Pinterest in conjunction with other social media on an ongoing basis in Chapter 9, but at this early stage, you might want to make an announcement on Facebook and Twitter that your business is now on Pinterest. Include a link to the Pinterest account so your fans and followers can see what you're up to. If you use a link shortener, such as bit.ly, you can track how many fans click through to Pinterest, which helps you evaluate where your Pinterest followers come from and which announcements were most effective.

> **PIN TIP**
>
> Add your Pinterest URL to your email signature to unobtrusively invite customers to visit your boards.

When you finish, click your web browser's back button to return to the Edit Profile screen, or choose **Settings** from the drop-down menu under your name.

Even if you signed up for Pinterest via Facebook, you can also link your Pinterest and Twitter accounts. Click the **Link to Twitter** radio button **ON** to join the two accounts.

To unlink your Pinterest and Facebook or Twitter accounts, click the radio button **OFF**. Doing this means you sign in with the email address and password you used when you created the account. If several people in your company pin to the Pinterest account, this is a way to limit what shows up on the business Facebook and Twitter accounts.

Appearing in Google Searches

Turn **Hide your Pinterest profile from search engines ON** if you don't want your Pinterest activity to appear in Google searches. Turn this button **OFF** if you do want to be appear in Google searches.

For marketing and search purposes, keep this **OFF**. Enabling your pins to appear in search engines means more eyes to your pins and your account.

Deactivating Your Account

We don't know why you'd ever want to do this, but if you want to delete your Pinterest account, click **Deactivate Account**. Just know that this wipes out your entire Pinterest identity, boards, pins, friends—everything. Unfortunately, this means that all content you have contributed will be deleted, which can be a very upsetting discovery for fans and followers you've cultivated on Pinterest. Deactivating doesn't delete your username and password, however, so if you want to reinstate your account at any time, you can do that by clicking the link in the email that Pinterest sends when you deactivate your account.

Remember to click **Save Profile** to save the changes you made to your profile. You can return to the Edit Profile screen whenever you want to make these changes. As Pinterest evolves, new options may appear that you'll want to use.

The Least You Need to Know

- Choose an account name that reflects your business so your customers can easily find you.
- Select categories to follow that interest your customers and apply to your business sector.
- Add the Pin It button to your web browser for quick and easy pinning.
- Use profile settings to manage who sees you and how.

Creating and Managing Your Boards

In This Chapter

- Understanding the Pinterest website
- Creating new boards
- Choosing a board category
- Collaborating and contributing to boards
- Describing your boards

After you set up your Pinterest account and profile, it's time to create your boards. (These are also sometimes called *pinboards*.) In this chapter, we tell you how to work with Pinterest boards.

There are essentially four tasks to do with boards: create the board, describe it, categorize it, and designate contributing pinners. We explain each of these tasks in the following sections. We talk about developing a board strategy in Chapter 7.

The Parts of Pinterest Web Pages

Before we begin, we want to be sure we're all on the same (web) page. Open the Pinterest home page by typing **pinterest.com** in the URL field of your browser. Or if you're already visiting Pinterest, click the Pinterest logo at the top of whatever page you're on. The Pinterest home page shows pins, which you view sorted by the tabs just under the logo:

- **Pinners you follow** shows the most recent pins made by pinners you follow.
- **Everything** displays the most recent pins made by everyone. The **Everything** menu lets you choose to view pins in a specific category.
- **Videos** displays the most recently pinned videos.
- **Popular** shows the most repinned pins.
- **Gifts** displays pins that have a price in the description, and a pull-down menu allows sorting by price range.

A short list of *engagement* other pinners had with your pins and boards appears in the **Recent Activity** box on the left side of your page. You may also see a **Friends to Follow** section. Just click the **Follow** button, and those friends' boards and pins appear when you click **Pinners you follow**. Any engagement they have with your boards and pins appears in the **Recent Activity** list, too. If you don't see the **Friends to Follow** section, click your name in the upper right to pull down the menu and click **Find Friends**. Click your browser's back button and then you'll see the **Friends to Follow** section.

DEFINITION

Engagement refers to any activity between a person and information online; for example, someone who's viewing Pinterest and following, liking, or repinning your pins.

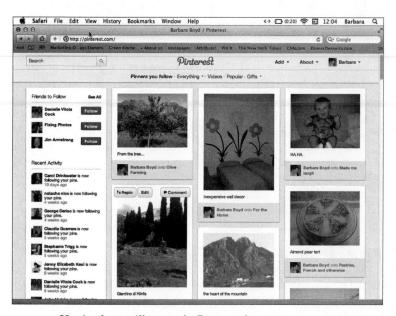

Here's what you'll see on the Pinterest home page.

We refer to parts of your Pinterest profile page throughout this chapter. To avoid confusion, take a moment to look at the following figure so you know what we mean when we refer to the *Pinterest toolbar* or *board thumbnail image*.

Your Pinterest profile page is where other pinners go to see your boards, as well as information about you and a list of the pins, repins, likes, comments, and follows you made most recently.

The Pinterest profile page.

Creating a New Board

During the account setup procedure, you created your initial boards, or confirmed the boards Pinterest suggested for you. However, you should add new boards on a regular basis to keep your customers and followers interested in your company or brand.

Every board should have an identity, theme, or focus, and new boards can reflect changes in your business, products, or services. For example, if you have an apparel brand, you want to add a board when the new season's items are available. You may want to tease customers with sketches before the actual designs are created. After the items are in stores, you could run a contest asking customers to pin photos on your board of how they're wearing your clothes.

At first glance, you might think that adding boards regularly works only for businesses that have obvious seasonal changes, such as fashion or car manufacturers. If you post to your blog on a regular basis or distribute a weekly or monthly email newsletter, you have a regular flow of information that can translate to boards. Think about how your business flows to identify happenings you want to communicate to your customers. See Chapter 7 for more ideas.

There are two ways to create new boards:

- Using the **Add** button on the Pinterest toolbar
- When pinning an image

To create a new board from any Pinterest web page, click the **Add** button on the Pinterest toolbar and then click **Create a Board**. The **Create a Board** dialog box opens. Click in the **Board Name** field, and type the name you want for the new board. Choose a category from the **Select a Category** pull-down menu.

You appear as the **Creator**, and you can let other people pin to the board by typing a name in the **Add another pinner** field. A list of names (of pinners you follow) that match the letters you type appears, and the choices narrow as you type more letters. When you see the name of the person you want to contribute to the new board, click that name and then click the **Add** button. Begin typing another name to add additional contributors. Click **Create Board**, and the board appears on your profile page.

Name, categorize, and add contributors when you create boards.

We show you how to add a board when pinning an image in Chapter 4, but for now, let's delve into each step in the board creation process to be sure you're getting the most marketing bang for your buck as you get started with Pinterest.

MARKETING MIX-UP

Do your best to name, describe, and categorize your board accurately, but don't worry if you change your mind later. You can always go back and edit any or all of this information.

Naming New Boards

The name of your new board can be as long as you like, but only up to 34 characters are displayed on the board thumbnail image on your profile page. If your name runs longer, the full name will appear when the board is open.

So why not keep it short and sweet? you might be thinking. The advantage to a longer name is that even if the entire name doesn't show up on the board on your profile, it's still searchable. If someone searches Pinterest for a word that's in the board name, even if it doesn't fit on your profile page, the board will still appear in the search results.

PIN TIP

Think about searchability when naming your board. Use your brand name and something that describes the type of content you plan to pin on the board, such as *Williams-Sonoma: Copper Cookware* rather than something more generic such as *pots and pans.*

Categorizing Your Board

Click the **Select a Category** pull-down menu to choose what category you want to assign to your new board. You can only assign one category to each board, so choose the category that best represents the images you pin on that specific board.

These categories are the same ones you see on the **Everything** pull-down menu on the Pinterest home page and the ones you selected from when you chose your interests during the Pinterest setup procedure. One of the ways people can discover your boards is by looking at boards in a specific category, which narrows the overwhelming choices that appear under **Everything**.

If your board fits in two different categories, such as Fitness and Sports, look at other boards in each category to see where your board would best fit in. You can also try one category and if you find you aren't reaching the audience you want or people just aren't following your board, you can try putting it in a different category to see if that increases interest. To change the category, click the **Select a Category** pull-down menu, scroll through until you find the category you want, and click it.

Pinterest prompts you to categorize an uncategorized board.

> **MARKETING MIX-UP**
>
> When you create a board while adding, creating, or repinning a pin, there isn't an option for categorizing. When you (or another pinner) first look at that new board, a message appears at the top asking you to choose a category. If someone else chooses a category for your board, you'll receive a message saying so. If you don't like the category another user selected for your board, you can change it by clicking **Edit** on the board.

Collaboration Versus Contribution

Another aspect of board management is deciding whether other people may contribute to your board, and if so, who and how many other users. *Collaborating* and *contributing* are two sides of the same coin.

In both cases, one person, referred to as the **Creator**, owns the board but many people can pin to it; the difference is in the planning. For example, you may want to collaborate on boards with other people in your company but invite customers to contribute to your boards. We explore collaboration strategies in Chapter 12, but for now, let's look at how to add contributors to your boards.

> **DEFINITION**
>
> **Collaborating** is when two or more parties work together toward a common goal and often generate ideas for one another. **Contributing** is when a pinner sees what's already established and adds to the existing content.

Choosing the Kingpinner

Within your company, you may have more than one pinner. There are two ways to approach this:

- Give multiple people access to one Pinterest account.
- Open multiple Pinterest accounts.

The advantage to having one Pinterest account many people can access is that all your boards are in one place, on one account. The downside is keeping everyone up to date on any password changes and the risk of renegade pinners if there are too many. The one account/multiple pinners scenario can probably work if you have four or fewer pinners who work closely together—for example, your marketing department manages your Pinterest account and each product manager manages a product board.

The alternative is to open multiple Pinterest accounts. Each account can represent a department or person within your company. When there's overlapping interest in a particular board, there are two options:

- One account creates the board and then adds the other account, or accounts, as a contributor with pinning privileges.
- Both accounts create boards and repin from each other.

For example, *Country Living* magazine has a Pinterest account and each editor has a separate account. Some images, such as the monthly magazine covers, are pinned by *Country Living*, whereas the editors often pin style images on their boards and *Country Living* repins them.

The second scenario has its advantages. Each account has one person who curates its identity, and the more contributors or repinning you have, the broader your possible following.

Whenever you create a new board, people who follow you will automatically follow the new board. If you're a contributor to a board, people who follow you will only see the boards you contribute to if they visit your profile, but they won't automatically follow the new board. That said, it makes sense to have the pinner with the most followers—or the type of followers you want to reach—create new boards and then make other pinners contributors.

Of course, all contributors will want to update their Facebook status or tweet the addition of new boards, which can generate a broader following. (We talk more about this in Chapter 11.)

Grant Pinning Privileges

You can establish who is allowed to pin to a board when you first create a board. If you decide after a board is created that you want to add contributors, go to the **Edit** screen by clicking **Edit** on the board to which you want to add a contributor or contributors.

The **Who can pin?** section shows who created the board and lets you choose who can pin images and videos to this board. If you do nothing, you are the only person who can pin to this board. If you want to let someone else pin to this board, too, type in the name of the person you want to give pinning privileges to. As you begin typing, a list of potential matches appears, and your choices are reduced as you type more letters of the name. When you see the name of the person you want to add, click it and then click **Add**.

> **MARKETING MIX-UP**
>
> You must follow at least one board of the person you want to add as a contributor to your board. If the name of the person you want to add doesn't appear in the list, you have to search Pinterest for that person, sign up to follow one of her boards, and go back to the **Edit** screen of your board and add the person.

The person you want to add as a contributor is notified by email that she has been invited to contribute to your board. Invitations appear at the top of your profile. Contributors' names appear on a board only after the invitation has been accepted. She can opt out immediately upon receipt of the invitation or directly from the board at a later date.

Contributors can invite other contributors, too. For example, Barbara can invite Christine to contribute to one of her boards and in turn, Christine can invite Pat to contribute to Barbara's board.

The board's Creator can delete any of the contributors. Contributors can only delete other contributors they invited. In our example, either Barbara or Christine can delete Pat, but Pat, unless she invites someone, can't delete anyone. To delete a contributor, click the **Edit** button under the thumbnail image of the board you want to work on, click the **X** next to the name of the contributor you want to delete, and click the **Remove** button in the dialog that appears.

The name of the pinner who sent the invitation appears next to the name of the invitee.

After you make your selections, click **Create Board** (or **Save Settings** if you're using the **Edit Board** function) and your new or edited board appears on your profile.

Editing Your Board Descriptions

You can leave your new board as is and immediately begin pinning, but we recommend you add a board description.

Because Pinterest is so visual, this opportunity to communicate with present and future customers is often overlooked. We're often surprised how few businesses write board descriptions. When people open one of your boards, the board description is another chance to tell a little about you and your business. The description should explain how the focus of the board ties in with your business offering. It's one of the many ways you can use Pinterest to reinforce brand identity and increase brand recognition. Remember, you want people who see your images to think of your brand and have a positive reaction to it.

Click **Edit Board** at the top of the empty board that opens as soon as you create a new board, or click **Edit** on the board thumbnail on your profile page. An **Edit Board/***board name* window opens with a few fields and options. You have a couple edit options here.

Change the Board Name

If you wish to change the name of the board, click in the **Title** field. Either select the text by clicking and dragging or click at the end of the text and use the Delete or Backspace key to remove the text. Retype or correct the board name.

Add a Description

The description appears under the board name when someone opens that board. There's a 500-character limit for board descriptions, but you can write a lot of information in that amount of space. Write a specific description that lets people who view this board know what they can expect to find pinned there.

> **PIN TIP**
>
> After you pin a few images, you can also designate a board cover—that's the large image shown on the thumbnail images of boards on your profile. It should be a compelling image that communicates the type of content pinned on that board. We show you how to change the board cover in Chapter 4.

Deleting Your Board

There may come a time when you want to delete a board. The most common scenario is when you create a board and pin one or two images but then decide it really doesn't fit with your marketing plan.

It makes a bigger, longer-lasting impact to have fewer active boards with frequently added pins than many boards with one or two pins.

To delete a board, click the **Edit** button under the board you want to delete, click **Delete Board** in the upper right, and click **Delete Board** again when asked if you're sure you want to delete the board (or click **Cancel** if you clicked **Delete Board** by mistake). Your board and all the pins on that board will be permanently erased from Pinterest's memory.

> **MARKETING MIX-UP**
>
> If you have products that are discontinued or no longer available, you may be tempted to delete a board that showcases those products. A better solution is to rename the board "No Longer Available" or "Discontinued Products." That way, you won't lose your search engine status, and although customers might not find exactly what they were looking for, they may find something new they want instead.

After you make the edits you want, click **Save Settings**. Click your browser's back, or previous page, button to return to the board, or choose **Boards** from the Profile Name menu.

> **PIN TIP**
>
> You can edit any of your boards at any time by clicking the **Edit** button underneath the board on your Pinterest **Boards** page.

The Least You Need to Know

- Create new boards to reflect changes in your business, which may be new products, new people, or seasonal offers.
- Consider searchability when naming boards and use words that describe the type of content followers will find.
- Choose your board's category appropriate to its content. If you're not getting the response you want, consider changing it.
- Add contributors to your boards to increase following and keep your boards varied.

Pinning to Your Boards

In This Chapter

- Easy pinning with the Pin It bookmarklet
- Making the best use of your pins
- Choosing pins for board covers
- Editing and updating your pins
- Interacting with other pinners
- Pinning from your iPhone

Now the pinning fun begins! As part of your marketing plan, you want to pin your own images but, in keeping with whole idea of Pinterest, you want to pin others' images, too. Of course, the other images may show your products, and that's all to your advantage, or they may depict a lifestyle that reflects your product line or service. The bottom line is that you want the pins on your boards to make viewers think of your company.

Pinning images is the main Pinterest activity. Pinning isn't limited to images or infographics, though. You also can pin videos, share links to blogs, and upload images. We show you a couple ways to pin from different sources in this chapter. What's more, you can take your pinning mobile with the Pinterest iPhone app, which we explain in this chapter, too. (Pinterest also released iPad and Android versions of its app in August 2012.)

Pinning Options

The important thing to remember when pinning from a website is to use an original source, or a *permalink*. Using original sources helps ensure the image owner is properly credited. A permalink, short for *permanent link*, is the URL that links to a specific story or post, as opposed to a link to the overall website or a single web page. Permalinks allow people to access the original image or the blog, article, instructions, etc. associated with the image.

Because you're using Pinterest for promotional and commercial purposes, you want to be sure you have permission to use the images you pin. At the time of writing, this is still a controversial area, and you'll want to check with your legal representative as to how to best handle the situation. This doesn't mean you can't use Pinterest; you just want to be on the up and up in how you use it.

Using the Pin It Bookmarklet

When you see an image on a website that you want to pin to one of your Pinterest boards, click the **Pin It** bookmarklet in the bookmarks or favorites bar of your browser. (If you haven't installed that yet, flip back to Chapter 2 for instructions.) All the pinnable images appear as thumbnails on the screen. Hover over the image you want to pin, and click **Pin This**.

A **Create Pin** dialog box opens. Choose the board you want to pin to from the pull-down menu, and type a description for your pin. The description can be up to 500 characters; the number next to the **Pin It** button displays how many letters remain for the description while you type. Click **Pin It**, and three buttons appear: **See your Pin**, **Tweet your Pin**, and **Share on Facebook**. Click one of these buttons, or wait a few seconds for the window to close by itself.

PIN TIP

Think about using specific keywords when describing your pins. That way, your pins will show up when other pinners search Pinterest. See Chapter 8 to learn more.

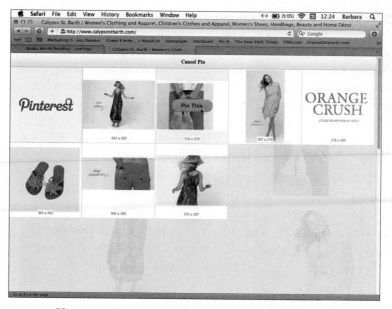

*Hover over the image you want to pin, and click **Pin This**.*

In some circumstances, the Pin It bookmarklet doesn't work. For example, you can't pin from Facebook, nor from some RSS feed programs like Google Reader. In these two cases, you can usually click through to the original blog or website and use the Pin It bookmarklet there. Other times a message appears that says no pinnable images were found, and some websites have opted to use a plug-in that blocks pinning from their site. If you absolutely must pin an image you find, try one of the procedures in the next two sections.

Adding a Pin

If you know the URL for a specific site that contains images you want to pin, you can add pins directly from the site by clicking **Add** and then **Add a Pin**. Type the URL where you want to search for images, and click **Find Images**.

The images available on that web page appear in the box to the left. Click the left and right arrows beneath the image to scroll through the available images. When you find an image you like, choose the board from the pull-down menu, type a description and tags, and click **Pin It**. Click the Twitter or Facebook buttons if you want to share your pin there. (We talk more about tags in Chapter 8.)

Uploading an Image

As part of your marketing plan, you want to upload your own images. If you have a lot of images on your computer—and who doesn't?—we suggest creating a folder that holds the images you want to upload to Pinterest or flagging them in your photo management application so you can find them easily when you're ready to upload the images to your boards.

To upload an image, click **Add** in the Pinterest toolbar, and click **Upload a Pin**. Click **Choose File**, and scroll through the directories and files on your computer until you find the image you want. Click the file, and click **Choose**. When your image appears in the **Upload a Pin** dialog box, click the pull-down menu to select the board to which you want to pin the image. Type a description, and click **Pin It**. Click the Twitter or Facebook buttons if you want to share your pin.

If you want to pin images on websites that don't support the Pin It bookmarklet, you can right-click or control-click to download the image file to your desktop and then upload it to Pinterest by following the previous steps. If you opt to do this, be sure to include the URL of the original image in the pin description so people who follow you can go to the original source.

VERY PINTERESTING!

Firefox, Chrome, Safari, or the latest version of Internet Explorer (IE9) are the recommended browsers for uploading images. You can upload high-resolution images, but Pinterest can't display in high-resolution so the quality will change after the file is uploaded.

When you upload an image, it doesn't automatically have a URL associated with it because the image came from your computer. You have to manually add a link in the **Edit Pin** window. We explain that in the "Editing Pins" section later in this chapter. Adding a watermark to your images is a good idea, not only to subtly reinforce your brand name but also to protect your products and copyright.

Pinning a Video

You can pin video from YouTube or Vimeo or pin an embedded YouTube or Vimeo video.

Open youtube.com, vimeo.com, or the web page with the embedded video and navigate to the video you want to pin. Click the **Pin It** bookmarklet, and follow the procedure as you would for pinning an image. A pinned video appears on the board where you pin it, in the category you assign to it, and on the **Videos** section accessible from the Pinterest home page.

VERY PINTERESTING!

You'll find a lot of websites sporting the **Pin It** button next to images and videos. Simply click the **Pin It** button, and proceed as you would if you'd clicked the Pin It bookmarklet.

Creating a Board While Creating a Pin

You may want to pin an image that doesn't quite fit the style or focus of any of your current boards. You can create a new board directly from the **Create Pin** or **Add a Pin** dialog box.

Simply scroll to the bottom of the list of boards and click **Create New Board**. Type a name for this board, and click **Pin It**. Click the Twitter or Facebook buttons if you want to share your pin, or click **Go to Pin** if you want to see it on the new board.

If you create a board from the **Create Pin** or **Add a Pin** window, you have to go to that board on your profile page and click **Edit** to choose a category from the pull-down menu.

Good Pins Versus Bad Pins

When Pinterest shot up in popularity in early 2012, a lot of controversy also shot up about copyright issues and whether repinning someone else's image, even with the original source, was copyright infringement. At the time of writing, a jury hasn't even been formed to legally decide where things stand; however, there are practices you can follow to stay on the right side of the law. We encourage you to review the Terms of Service (pinterest.com/about/terms) and to speak with your company's legal adviser if you have any questions or concerns.

A good pin gives credit where credit is due, whereas a bad pin can result from mindless pinning or, worse yet, intentional plagiarism. Bad pins can be as innocent as pinning a photo you like from a website and crediting the website for the photo rather than the photographer. The other end of the bad pin spectrum shows up in the craft business, where one person copies another's original craft idea and pins the resulting object or product as his own. It's fine to show what you've made, but give credit to the inventor if it's a copy of something. If you pin the copied creation without adding a *hat tip*, you're perpetuating plagiarism.

DEFINITION

A **hat tip** is a virtual tip of your hat to someone who spurred an idea or creation. A movement is in motion to use two attribution symbols: ∽ or the word *via* for direct reference and ⤳ or the words *hat tip* for hat tip.

When a single pinner makes these mistakes, they might be overlooked or the pinner may lose followers. As a business, you can't risk the type of negative press that can result from irresponsible pinning. The following sections outline tactics to follow to always keep your pins in the good pins category.

Images and videos pinned (or embedded) from Flickr, YouTube, Vimeo, and Behance have an automatically determined, uneditable attribution under the pin, which links to the original work, the author, and the hosting provider. If the pin is repinned, the attribution remains. Attributions cannot be edited, although the link itself can be. Links point to where you found the content, and the content may appear in different places, whereas attribution indicates the service where the author posted the item.

Pinning from Original Sources

An original source can be an image of which you own the copyright. When you commission photographers to photograph your products and the people who work for you, or designers to create ad campaigns and marketing materials, be sure the rights you purchase include online promotion and distribution.

An original source image can also be a snapshot of a customer, wearing your scarf, who ideally has signed a release that you can use the photo, or he pinned it and you repinned it. But what happens when it's a fashion magazine that runs a spread about winter fashions and your scarf is among the products shown? Pin the image, but pin it directly from the magazine's website. Don't scan the image from the magazine and upload it as if you had arranged the photo shoot.

PIN TIP

To find the original source for an unidentified image, open google.com and click the **Images** tab. Open the folder, or a separate web window, where the image exists, and click and drag the image just under the search field on Google. A dialog box opens that instructs you to **Drop image here**. Release the mouse or trackpad button to release the image in that box. Google searches and gives you a list of matches with the sources.

Pinning from Permalinks

When someone clicks a pin on one of your boards or on one of the Pinterest home page views, a new window opens with an enlarged image. You also see the pin's caption, the board it's on, who originally pinned it and from where, and who has repinned or liked the pin.

*Clicking the thumbnail of a pin opens a larger image
with more information about the pin.*

When you click the enlarged image, the URL associated with the
image opens. The URL can be one of the following:

- The website from which the image was pinned using the
  Pin It bookmarklet.
- The link you added when you edited an uploaded pin's
  description.

Either of these can be a permalink. Think about your customer's
experience if you decide not to use a permalink. For example, if
you have items from a catalog, you probably want to link to the
individual web pages that display each item (permalink), not to
your general web catalog (nonpermalink). Permalinks take a viewer
directly to the original image. That's where you want them to go.

VERY PINTERESTING!

Permalinks also help you move up the search engine status ladder,
which enhances your search engine optimization efforts in the long run.

Repinning

Often while browsing Pinterest, you see something on someone else's board that you'd like to have on your board. You copy that image to your board by *repinning* it. The good thing about repinning is that the original pinner is credited and the pin maintains the original source link, no matter how often it's repinned. However, you should be sure the link meets the criteria for a good pin before repinning.

You can repin in two ways:

- Hover over the thumbnail view of the pin and click **Repin**.
- In full-size view, click **Repin** in the top-left corner.

Complete the repin as you would a new pin. First, choose the board where you want to repin the pin. Next, edit the description. By default, the description written by the original pinner appears, but you can change it. Select to share it on Facebook or Twitter if you like and then click **Repin**.

> **MARKETING MIX-UP**
>
> If you find someone is pinning your copyrighted images or registered trademarks, you can file a complaint with Pinterest following the instructions outlined at pinterest.com/about/copyright and pinterest.com/about/trademark.

Editing Pins

Although you type in the description of a pin when you create it, you may want to change the information or even move the pin to a different board later. To do this, go to your profile page and open the board that contains the pin you want to edit, or click the **Pins** tab to see all your pins. You can then access the Edit Pin dialog box from the thumbnail view or full-size view. In thumbnail view, hover the mouse over the pin and click **Edit**. In full-size view, which opens when you click the thumbnail view, click **Edit** in the top-left corner.

Click the description field to add to or change the pin description. Click the pull-down category menu to change the pin's category. Click **Save** when you finish making edits.

Adding a URL to a Pin

You want your customers to find your website, so your pins should link to your website—ideally to the webpage where the image resides. The easiest way to accomplish this is to pin images directly from your website. If, instead, you upload images that aren't on your website or blog, you can still add a URL to the pin.

Hover your mouse over the pin you want to add a URL to, and click the **Edit** button. Click in the **Link** field and type the URL (or go to the web page and copy and paste the URL). When someone clicks through your pin, the URL you added will open.

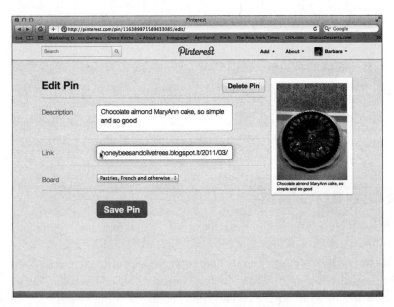

Add a URL to images you upload to link the pin to your website.

Adding a Price to a Pin

The Gifts category of Pinterest is a great place to show off your wares and services—after all, that's where people with the intention to buy go to look for great gift ideas. Adding a price to your pin automatically places a copy of the pin here. The pin appears in the price range category that's appropriate to the price you entered.

If your pins show products, you want to have the pin link to a catalog on your website, and you should also put a price on the pin. To include the price, type the $ or £ symbol followed by the amount in the description. As Pinterest becomes more international, we can only surmise that you'll be able to use other monetary symbols in the future.

MARKETING MIX-UP

Pins with price tags are added frequently, and there's a delay between the time you pin the item and when it appears in the Gifts section. So don't panic if you don't see your pin right away.

Interacting with Other Pinterest Users and Pins

While you're pinning and repinning, you probably flip through other boards and pins. Living vicariously through boards is one of the pleasures of Pinterest. As with other social media forums, you can—and should!—interact with other users on Pinterest, especially to promote your business.

Mentioning Another Pinterest User

You can refer to another Pinterest user in either your pin description or in a comment (which we explain in the "Commenting on Pins" section coming up). You have to follow at least one board that belongs to the user you want to mention. If you know potential clients who use Pinterest, this is a way to do some very direct marketing. For example, if you're a graphic designer, you might want to send a pin that shows an idea to a potential client who uses Pinterest. People who follow the pinner you mention will see your pin, too, which expands your brand's reach.

To mention a user, type the @ symbol right before the user's name. A list of potential matches appears and choices diminish as you type more letters. Click the name of the user you want to mention. The user will receive a notification that you've mentioned him.

> **PIN TIP**
>
> If other pinners @mention you, an **@mentions** tab appears on your profile page next to the other viewing tabs.

Liking a Pin

If you see a pin you like, hover over the thumbnail image on the board and click **Like**. Or on the full-size image, click **Like** in the upper-left corner. When you like a pin, a notification appears in the **Recent activity** list on the **Pinners You Follow** page of the person who pinned the pin, and a thumbnail image of your profile photo appears at the bottom of the full-size image window.

If at some point you want to remove a like, click the **Likes** tab on your profile page and click **Unlike** on any pin you want to eliminate. When you refresh the page, the unliked pins will be removed.

You can find a list of likes others have placed on your pins in the **Recent activity** list of **Pinners You Follow** section of the Pinterest home page, which you access from the main Pinterest web page. You can see all your likes (or those of other pinners) by clicking **Likes** at the top of your (or other pinners') profile page.

> **PIN TIP**
>
> Some pinners use the like function to put a bookmark on items they might want to repin later or until they have enough similar items to create their own board. Because you don't want to repin everything, this gives you an opportunity to thoughtfully curate boards, which we talk about in depth in Chapter 10. You can always remove likes later if you want.

Commenting on Pins

People who view your boards and pins can make comments, and you can make comments on other Pinterest users' pins you view. As with likes, you can comment on the thumbnail image by hovering over the image and clicking **Comment** in the upper-right corner or on the full-size image by typing in the **Add a comment** field.

When someone comments on your pins, a notification appears in the **Recent activity** list on the **Pinners You Follow** section of the Pinterest home page. The comments also appear on the pins themselves.

Be sure you read through the comments and respond, even briefly, to establish a relationship. Just saying "Thank you" can often be enough. If you want to mention another Pinterest user in a comment, use the @ symbol before his name, as explained previously. If you repin an image and you want the user to know, it's nice to put the pinner's name with an @ in the comments so he receives a notification of the repin.

You can delete comments you make or others make on your pins. Click the thumbnail image of the pin to enlarge it, and click the **X** to the right of the comment you want to delete. You can't edit comments, so if you want to change a comment, you must delete it and type a new one.

> **PIN TIP**
>
> You can't delete comments others make on other pins, but if you find something you feel is spam, inappropriate, or hateful, you can report it by clicking the flag icon to the right of the comment.

Messages from other pinners—such as likes, comments, follows, or contributor activations—appear in the list next to your profile picture on your profile page. However, you can't scroll backward through the history of this section, so some messages might be overwritten by newer ones. If you turn on **Email Settings** in the **Notifications** section of the **Edit Profile** window, you'll receive an email message that contains the entire message along with a link you can use to reply to the sender.

Using the Pinterest App

If you use an iPhone or iPad, or an Android smartphone or tablet, the Pinterest app gives you another way to manage your account and pin images to your boards. The Pinterest app is a great way to maintain your pinning activity when you're away from the office or when you see something you immediately want to add to one of your boards. Although working with your pins, boards, followers, and followees is pretty much the same on all apps, there are a few differences on the iPad app. Here we first explain the iPhone and Android app, and at the end of this section, we point out the differences in the iPad app.

You can download the Pinterest app through the iTunes Store for iOS devices and at https://play.google.com for the Android version. Even better: it's free!

Understanding the App Icons on iPhone or Android

When you tap the Pinterest app icon on the home screen, you then log in with your email address and password or your Facebook or Twitter account name and password. The iPhone and Android app have a similar interface: five buttons run across the bottom of the Pinterest app screen. Tapping each produces a specific action.

Following displays the most recent pins placed by the pinners you follow. Scroll up to move through the images, and scroll down to see the app buttons. Tap the image to open the pin, and then tap **Repin** or **Like** beneath the image or tap the **Action** button (the arrow shooting out of a box) to share, save, or email the pin. Scroll to the bottom of the pin to leave a comment. As with the web version of Pinterest, tapping an open pin takes you to the original source. Tap the **Back** button (the left-pointing arrow) in the upper-left corner to return to the Pinterest app Following screen.

Explore opens the Pinterest category list. Tap a category to see pins in that category, or tap the **Search** field to find a specific pin, board, or person. Interact with pins as explained in the previous section on following.

Camera, as you might guess, takes a photo and pins it to one of your boards. We explain this more in the next section.

News shows who has recently started following you or liked, commented on, or repinned one of your pins. Tap someone who has started following you to see that pinner's profile. Tap a like, comment, or repin to see the respective pin and either repin, delete, comment on, or share it. Tap the **Back** button or one of the buttons at the bottom of the screen to return to the **News** list.

Profile lets you view your Pinterest profile. More on this in a few sections.

Using the Camera with Pinterest

Tap the **Camera** button at the bottom of the Pinterest screen to take a photo of something you want to pin to one of your Pinterest boards. Maybe you just spotted someone sporting something from your newest line of clothing and you want to pin it *now* rather than wait until you get back to the office.

Here's how to upload a snapshot from your smartphone:

1. Tap the **Camera** button. The image shows up on your smartphone.

2. Tap the **Camera** button to take the photo or tap the **Photos** button (the stacked squares in the lower-right corner) to choose a photo that already resides on your smartphone.

3. The **Pin It!** screen opens.

4. Tap the **Describe your pin...** field to type in a description.

5. Tap **Choose a Board** to open the **Choose a Board** screen, which lists your boards.

6. Tap the name of the board where you want to pin the photo, or add a new board by typing a name in the **Create a new board** field and then tap **Create**.

7. If you want to share the pin on Facebook or Twitter, tap one or both of those buttons and type in the appropriate account information.

8. Tap **Pin It** in the upper-right corner when you're finished. A progress bar appears as the image is loaded. A message tells you when your image is pinned, and the image appears on the **Pinned** screen.

PIN TIP

You can share your pin on Facebook and/or Twitter at any time after you pin the image by choosing **Share** on the full-size pin view window.

Viewing Your Boards and Pins

You can view your boards, pins, and likes on the app by tapping **Profile**, then tapping the appropriate **Boards**, **Pins**, or **Likes** tab. Tap a board from the **Boards** list to see the board and then tap a pin on the board to see the pin. Tap a specific pin from the **Pins** list to see it. From any of the three lists, when you tap through to the single pin level, you can tap in the empty field at the bottom of the screen and type in a comment or tap **Repin**, **Delete**, or the **Action** button to apply any of those actions to your pin.

Tap the **Followers** tab to see who is following you. Tap the **Following** tab to see who you are following, and tap a specific name in the list to view that pinner's boards. On either list, tap **Follow** or **Unfollow** next to each name to take that action.

Tapping the **Account** button (it looks like a gear) in the upper-left corner gives you five options:

- **Account Settings**, which opens, and lets you edit, your account settings in the same manner as on the website, which is explained in Chapter 2
- **Pinterest Support**, which opens the Pinterest help topics and gives you the option of sending a help request directly to Pinterest

- **Terms and Privacy**, where you can read all the Pinterest legalese

- **Logout**, which logs you out of Pinterest

- **Cancel**, which you tap if you decide you don't want to do any of the above tasks

Using the iPad App

There are two major differences between the smartphone app and the iPad app: there's no camera function that allows taking photos with the iPad and pinning them directly to Pinterest, and there's an in-app web browser. The buttons have the same functions, but you find them in slightly different locations. You access all the buttons from a sidebar that opens when you swipe from left to right on the iPad screen or tap the **List** button in the upper-left corner. Note these differences:

- **News** is opened by tapping the button in the upper right of the sidebar. The icon shows two pushpins in a dialog bubble.

- **Account** is opened by tapping the button at the bottom right of the sidebar—again, it looks like a gear. There is no cancel button, so just tap elsewhere on the screen if you've opened this menu by mistake.

- **Profile** opens when you tap your name at the bottom of the sidebar.

- **Following** opens the most recent pins of pinners you follow.

- **Browse the Web** opens a Pinterest-specific web browser. Type the URL for the website you want to pin from in the **Go to this address** field. A nifty tool shows thumbnails of images that have recently been pinned from the site you're viewing, and tapping the **Pin It** button displays pinnable images found on the site. Tap any image and pin as explained previously in this chapter.

- **Search** lets you look for specific pins, boards, or people.
- Tapping a category from the list shows you the most recent pins in that category.

VERY PINTERESTING!

Syncing bookmarks between your computer and iPad will make the Pin It button show up on Safari (you find it by tapping the **Bookmarks** button and then choosing **Bookmarks Bar**) on the iPad, which is handy if you're surfing the web outside the Pinterest browser and find something you want to pin. However, you have to sign in to Pinterest from Safari for this to work.

The Least You Need to Know

- Use the Pin It bookmarklet to pin images from the web, including your own images so they link back to your website and help build your search engine status.
- Always use primary sources and permalinks so the rightful image owner is credited.
- Pin videos from YouTube and Vimeo to add variety to your boards. Attributions appear automatically when you pin from YouTube, Vimeo, Flickr, and Behance.
- Interact with other pinners with likes and comments, and remember to thank pinners who like and comment on your pins.
- Use the iPhone, iPad, or Android app to pin things you see while you're out and about.

Pinning Down Your Marketing Strategy

Strategy is key to every part of your business plan, and marketing is no exception. Part 2 leads you through the steps to create a Pinterest marketing plan. We ask questions to make you think about where you want your business to go and how you expect Pinterest to help you get there. The tools we present are Pinterest specific, although you can apply some of the ideas to your overall online marketing plan.

Chapters 5 and 6 talk about establishing Pinterest goals that support your business goals. Chapter 7 explains how to curate boards that support your brand and best tell your story, and Chapter 8 explores each part of a pin and the opportunity it offers to showcase your product or service or connect with your customer.

In all four chapters, we present examples of how businesses from different sectors and of different sizes are using Pinterest to increase their customer base and revenues. And we give you practical, hands-on tools to create a winning pinning strategy.

Developing a Marketing Strategy

In This Chapter

- Establishing your marketing goals for Pinterest
- Coming up with a plan
- Choosing the perfect pinner
- Reaching your customers

If you're a small business owner, reaching your customer base is probably your number-one priority. After all, without your customers, you're out of business. But how do you let potential customers know you exist? You need a marketing and public relations plan. Maintaining a constant Pinterest presence can be a key part of both.

You want to reach new customers, but it's just as important to keep in touch with your existing customers. Repeat business takes less work than finding new customers, and although you shouldn't rely on repeat business for 100 percent of your client base, it should be between 40 and 60 percent of your business. Existing clients or customers can be your best source for finding and procuring new customers, and testimony from satisfied customers is often the best way to convince new customers to work with you.

Whether your have an existing marketing plan or you fly by the seat of your pants, in this chapter, we guide you through the steps to including Pinterest in your marketing and public relations efforts.

Setting Your Pinterest Goals

Even if you've never written a specific marketing plan, you have goals for your business. Generating more revenue by finding more customers is a common goal, but it's not the *only* goal. You may want to offer more innovative products or augment your online business with store representation. If you offer a service, perhaps you want your existing customers to rely on you for a more expanded offering. One of your objectives may be to support your favorite nonprofit through a business campaign.

By keeping your general business goals in mind, you can begin to clarify specific Pinterest goals. The following table shows how Pinterest could support each of the previously mentioned goals.

Integrating Business Goals with Pinterest Goals

Business Goal	Pinterest Goal
Increase revenue	Increase brand awareness to increase customer base
Gain store representation	Collaborate with stores
Increase per-client spending	Highlight lesser-known services
Support a nonprofit	Run a donation-with-purchase campaign

So what are your business and/or marketing goals, and what Pinterest goals would support them?

The preceding examples are specific, and we encourage you to think in this way, but you should come up with some of your own goals.

Later in this chapter, we elaborate on broad Pinterest goals and give examples of boards and pins that reflect that type of goal. In subsequent chapters, we explore in depth the tactics for implementing them.

Defining Your Customer

You can increase revenue in three principle ways:

- Increase your customer base
- Increase each per-purchase total
- Increase your prices

Although the third can be a valid tactic, Pinterest is better used for the first two.

One of the first Pinterest goals that comes to mind is attracting new customers by developing a following. On the surface, you might think a bigger following means more business and therefore more revenue, but you should think about quality versus quantity. If you have 500,000 followers but they're all lookers as opposed to buyers, you aren't really increasing your customer base. You want to reach the buying customer and the *influencers*.

DEFINITION

An **influencer** is a Pinterest user who has a lot of followers who look to her for advice and suggestions. An influencer influences her followers' buying decisions.

To identify influencers, however, first you have to identify your customer or client. The following table gives you some questions you should think about to define your ideal customer or client, whether an individual or company.

Who Is Your Customer?

Individual Customer	Business-to-Business Customer
Where does she live?	Where is the business?
How old is she?	How old is the company?
What's her economic standing?	What's the company's revenue or worth?
Does she have a family?	What's the company's size?
What does she do for fun?	What sector is it in?
What is her lifestyle?	What's the company culture?
What problem does your product or service solve?	What problem does your product or service solve?
How will your client use your product or service?	How will your client use your product or service?
How does she make decisions, and who does she look to for decision-making advice?	Who are the key stakeholders and decision-makers?

Come up with more questions—and answers—specific to your product or service. With the answers to these questions, you can put yourself in your client's frame of mind and begin thinking about how to communicate with him and build a relationship.

Who Are the Influencers You Want to Reach?

Influencers help your business by doing the following:

- Passing the word along about you/your business, either through connections or media outlets
- Instilling confidence in your product or service
- Setting trends

Lisa Barone of Outspoken Media (smallbiztrends.com/2010/07/the-5-types-of-influencers-on-the-web.html) defines 5 types of influencers, while Klout (klout.com) identifies 12 types in its Influence Matrix.

Pins and repins of your images and brand meet all three of the influencer's tasks, and ideally, you reach a point on Pinterest where you have many followers who do both. Just like you want to create a mix of media outlets to promote your brand, you want a mix of influencer types to spread the word about you. The very nature of Pinterest, combined with the number of followers a pinner can acquire, makes finding influencers an important part of determining who you want to reach.

To select influencers, take some time to look around the Pinterest boards in categories related to your business. Take note of images you like and pinners whose names you see repeatedly. Look at the profiles of frequently seen pinners, and note how many followers they have. Influencers usually have a large following, their pins are often repinned, and their individual pins contain a lot of "likes" and comments.

MARKETING MIX-UP

The nature of social media brings an unusual—and growing—problem known as "false influence." On Pinterest, this happens when an established influencer repins a noninfluencer's work and the noninfluencer is subsequently flooded with follows.

Think of how you interview a potential employee; looking at the quality of a pinner's pins is like looking at a résumé. The pins tell you a lot about her interests and aesthetic. Look to see if she's pinning from original sources or repinning. If you see a lot of repinning, go a level deeper and look at the pinners she repins from. Both pinners and repinners can be effective influencers.

Once you've identified potential influencers, begin following them or even ask if they would like to contribute to one or more of your boards. (We talk about collaborating in Chapters 3 and 12.)

The influencer is subtle, and sometimes she doesn't even know she's an influencer. But as with all social media, the influencer is a key element in your marketing plan.

Quality Versus Quantity Following

Now that you have identified your ideal customer's profile, think about how many customers you need to reach your revenue goal. 100? 1,000? Maybe only 10. The expected rate of return on direct-mail campaigns falls between 0.5 and 2 percent, which means to procure 10 customers, you need to reach out to at least 500 people for a 2 percent return, or as many as 2,000 for a 0.5 percent return. In turn, for 100 customers, you need to reach between 5,000 and 20,000, and for 1,000, your reach has to be between 50,000 to 200,000.

Print, television, and radio advertising greatly increase your reach-out to potential buyers—plus a bunch of other people who probably aren't interested in your products or services. Direct mail, by definition, is targeted to potential buyers.

Unlike television and radio advertising, which can be missed because the viewer or listener gets up for a drink or channel surfs when the commercials come on, a viewer consciously goes to a social media page. Even here, Pinterest is different. Facebook or Google ads can quite easily be ignored, whereas pins aren't relegated to the sidelines. They're mixed together and divided only by category—separate yet equal. The categorical divisions work to your advantage because you find followers and pinners who are already interested in what you have to offer.

Marketing, or what we consider *passive* or *subtle advertising*, on social media platforms in general but especially on Pinterest, falls somewhere between direct mail—quality—and broad-based advertising—quantity. What's more, Pinterest brings you qualified traffic because your followers are already interested in your products, making your pins relevant and interesting. What's more, those followers probably have a lot of your desired customer profile traits.

 DEFINITION

Passive advertising is a marketing tactic that keeps your name or brand and products or services in front of potential customers. On Pinterest, you accomplish this with your boards and your pins on other pinners' boards. The message isn't "Buy our stuff!" but "Look what we do!"

So how many Pinterest followers do you want to reach? The question you could ask yourself when setting this Pinterest goal is whether you want to use Pinterest as a direct-mail tool or a general advertising tool. The beauty is that you can do both. You can build different boards to accomplish each task and consider setting a following goal for each board.

Next we talk about the type of goal you might associate with different kinds of boards. Bear in mind that the goals are not mutually exclusive, and often multiple boards and multiple goals overlap.

Increasing Brand Awareness

Psychologically speaking, we tend to gravitate to things that are familiar to us. That said, when something becomes too familiar, we tend not to notice it anymore—or worse yet, it falls into the "familiarity breeds contempt" category. Pinterest gives you the opportunity to maintain a brand presence that's visually different each time, and because Pinterest is more fluid and dynamic, the risk of breeding contempt is lower.

Clearly, increasing brand awareness falls into the general advertising category. Before a potential customer buys from you, she has to know about you or your brand. With this goal, you focus on the quantity of pinners. The more people who see your brand and see it frequently, the more likely they are to either buy from you or talk about your brand to others. In fact, one of the most effective ways to increase brand awareness is through influencers who pin or repin images of you, your products, or your company on their boards, as we explained in the section "Who Are the Influencers You Want to Reach?"

Let's look at an example. Vivid Lime is a digital marketing agency just beginning to curate a Pinterest presence. You can see in the following figure they're on the right track because they've created boards that showcase the company, the staff, and their clients.

*Company and employee images can be an important part
of a brand awareness campaign.*
(Vivid Lime [Strategic Digital Marketing], vividlime.com)

Attracting New Customers

If more than 60 percent of your revenue comes from existing
customers, you want to spend some of your marketing efforts on
procuring new customers.

The question to ask is whether you want more of the type of
customers you already have or if you want to expand into a new
market. Once you know what type of new customer you want to
attract, you can tailor your boards to that audience. For example, if
you make rustic stools that you typically market to people interested
in country décor but you use original designs that offer a modern
twist, you could create a board that showcases your stools in unusual
settings along with modern art images that influence your design.

By categorizing this board in Design rather than Home Decor, you
reach out to a different audience.

Increasing Product Awareness

This goal ties in with both business goals of increasing revenue through new customers and increasing the per-purchase total with existing customers. It correlates to a direct-mail strategy. Your boards show your products, and the followers for those boards should be first and foremost your existing customers who perhaps aren't familiar with your entire product line or service offering.

This board from Kaufman Mercantile is a good example of highlighting products, which are home and garden sundries, including office supplies pictured here, along with lifestyle images where their products could be used.

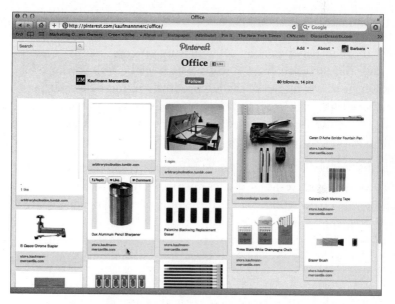

*Great photos introduce customers to your product and
keep them coming back to see more.*
(overall board: www.kaufmann-mercantile.com; top row, third
image indoor by Manoteca, Elisa Cavani; top row, fourth image
Anna Lilja Creative)

Notice the quality of the product photos. This is a company that sells chalk, staplers, erasers, and pencils, but because of the photos, which showcase the products' form and function, we want to buy them all. These images present the idea behind their brand. Check out their Garden and Kitchen boards, too, for other great examples.

Engaging with Customers

Social media is about engaging and sharing. You pin your images or images that portray the lifestyle or feeling your products and services support. Your existing and potential customers follow you because they enjoy looking at these pins and turn to you, your products, and services to obtain that lifestyle or feeling.

One way to show potential customers that your products and services will make their lives better is to invite existing customers to share their experience by collaborating on your boards. Their sharing reinforces their own positive experience with your products and services, which makes them more likely to increase their per-purchase totals on repeat business. You can solicit feedback from those same customers by creating boards that request their input and collaboration, as we discuss in Chapter 12.

Country Living has a contest board (pinterest.com/countryliving/contests-sweepstakes) that invites customers (their readers) to create a Pinterest board, upon which all the pins have to be tagged with *#countryliving* and *#dreambedroom*, for the bedroom contest, or *#dreamporch*, for the porch contest. Asking customers to contribute to your boards instills customer identification and engagement with your brand.

This was social media marketing genius because the *hashtag* (which you can learn more about in Chapter 8) made the keywords searchable, driving traffic to both *Country Living*'s website and Pinterest boards. This type of collaboration turns your customers into advertising outlets.

DEFINITION

Hashtag refers to a word or phrase preceded by the hash or pound symbol (#). Hashtags make the word or phrase searchable, making it a keyword. Hashtags are mostly used on social media platforms to create conversations or exchanges about a specific topic.

Becoming the Niche Expert

In addition to gravitating to the familiar, we like to align ourselves with experts whom we admire. Experts instill a sense of trust and reassurance. Similar to influencers, experts do the dirty work for us. An expert goes through the trial-and-error phases of a practice, experiencing the failure that leads to success and allowing us to take advantage of that success without living the disappointment of the failures.

By becoming the expert in your niche, you create a following of customers and influencers. Create pins and boards that showcase the process, and honestly communicate the near-misses that are testimony to the veracity of your experience. Who would you trust more: someone who succeeded on the first try without any effort, or someone who tried different avenues to come up with the best solution?

Consider creating a testimony board that lends truth to your expert claims or a question-and-answer board with creatively fashioned pins.

Covington Aircraft created a board that represents aircraft engine overhaul. Each pin links to a blog or video that highlights one of their in-house experts or a project that attests to their expertise. In keeping with Pinterest style, even for someone who isn't interested in aircraft maintenance, the images are attractive and eye-catching.

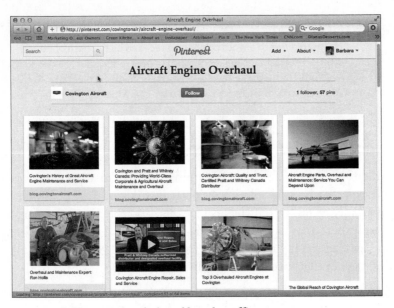

*Pin images or links to blogs that affirm your expert
standing.*
(Covington Aircraft)

Offering an Alternative to Customer Support

Pinterest's video capabilities let you create a customer support
alternative. You have customer support FAQs and contact information on your website, which your specific pins should link to.
Infographics are popular—and frequently repinned—so use them
as an opportunity to present step-by-step solutions in a visually
interesting way, be it a chart, a graph, or a photo and typographical
treatment.

Offering an alternative to traditional customer-support channels
reinforces your image as a complete and caring product and service
provider.

Increasing Traffic and Sales

While each of the previous goals indirectly supports the ultimate objective of increasing traffic and sales, you may want to make this a specific Pinterest goal and apply tactics to meet it.

It's great if more people recognize your brand and product and the press talks about you, but if you want to specifically increase traffic to your website and augment your sales revenues, you want to include incentives on your Pinterest pins and boards.

A subtle incentive is the inclusion of the price of an item on the pin. More engaging and less subtle are campaigns that entice customers to interact, such as contests, virtual scavenger hunts, coded discounts, and limited-time offers. For example, if you have an overstock of an item, you can visually promote it on Pinterest with a fabulous image along with a pin caption that invites viewers to go to your website and take advantage of a Pinterest discount. These types of promotions also help you determine where your customer base comes from.

Generating Media Coverage

Pinterest is quickly becoming a go-to site for spotting trends. If generating media coverage is one of your business goals, Pinterest can help your brand get discovered by popular media outlets that scan Pinterest for content.

Read Chapters 7, 8, 10, and 12 for tips on creating boards and pins that attract media coverage. As part of your public relations program, you want to let media outlets that follow you know you have a Pinterest presence.

VERY PINTERESTING!

You may have noticed news coverage of videos or tweets that go viral— that is, they spread exponentially through the social media channels. This gives new meaning to Marshal McLuhan's famous quote: "The medium is the message." (*Understanding Media: The Extensions of Man,* 1964)

Developing Your Plan

Typically, there are two types of marketing plans: waterfall and agile. A waterfall plan is the traditional marketing plan that focuses on long-term goals; repeats familiar, strategic programs; and is often costly. An agile plan works on short-term, measurable goals with low-cost programs applied to various media that are expanded when proven successful. In waterfall marketing, the brand is imposed by the strategy, whereas in agile marketing, the brand evolves from client interaction.

Given the present-day media options, agile and waterfall marketing plans don't have to be exclusive. In fact, tactics taken from each can be complementary, and many marketing plans take advantage of both styles.

From our point of view, Pinterest can be incorporated into either marketing style, and sometimes used for both simultaneously. The waterfall style is most often utilized by large corporations with big budgets and numerous staff members. Agile, which is inspired by the agile project management system software developers use, works well in smaller companies with team members who often have multiple roles. Agile is short term, task oriented, and measurement driven. Waterfall is about long-term strategy and tactics. That said, you can probably imagine how short-term agile tactics can support a long-term waterfall strategy.

Pinterest Marketing Diamond

After you set your Pinterest objectives in association with your business goals, think about how you're going to reach those targets. In this section, we share a tool we developed to help you visualize your intentions and the number and types of boards that will help you meet your goals.

We used the goals outlined earlier in this chapter, although your goals may be different. Brand awareness is at the top point, and the bottom point is customer support. Objectives run horizontally across the diamond, and the width reflects the proportion of boards applied to each one. In the middle, the widest section that runs from the left and right points is where you and your customer meet at your product or service offerings. This is the intention for which the most boards would be created.

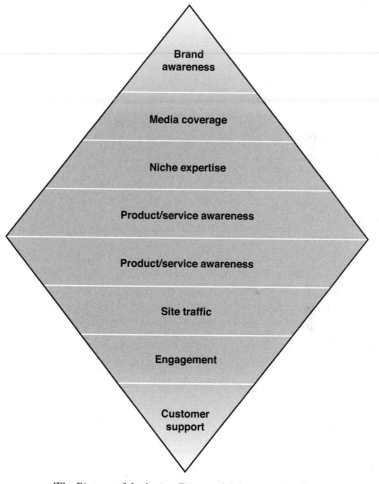

The Pinterest Marketing Diamond helps you visualize your goals and plan the boards that will support your marketing plan.

Goal Worksheet

Goals are somewhat ephemeral, and quantifying each one makes the tasks it will take to achieve that goal clearer. For each objective, we suggest you create a *mind map* or outline, whichever format you're more comfortable with, that answers the following questions:

- What is my goal?
- What do I physically need to achieve the objective?
- How will I meet those needs? Do I have to create the items? Does someone else have them? Or where can I find them?
- How long will it take to meet my goal?
- How can I measure my success?
- Are there next steps or maintenance to consider?

DEFINITION

Mind mapping is a way to visually and conceptually organize and generate ideas to brainstorm in an attempt to solve problems, make decisions, and solidify plans. The key concept or problem is at the center, and ideas extend outward in hub and spoke style, but they can also be connected to each other. Mind mapping software is available, but all you really need is pencil and paper.

Here's an example of how your responses might look:

What is my goal? Create a niche expertise presence on Pinterest by creating two boards showing our company infrastructure, one for the corporate staff and one for the engineering staff, and creating collaborative boards with at least three clients who agree to offer testimonials.

What do I physically need to build boards that help me achieve that objective? Photos and bios of the team. Photos of client success. (From their websites? Get release forms.)

How will I meet those needs? Do I have to create the items? Does someone else have them? Or where can I find them? Use photos and bios from our public relations files. Consider shooting newer photos. Contact clients for collaborative boards.

How long will it take to meet my goal? Two weeks for the internal boards and one month for the collaborative client boards.

How can I measure my success? Boards are created and pinned within one month. At least one story placed in media outlet that reaches our customer base.

Are there next steps or maintenance to consider? Continue adding success stories and testimonials introducing our clients to Pinterest and stimulating collaborative effort. Add video from our engineering team members.

Patience Is a Virtue

One of the key things to keep in mind with Pinterest is the time it takes to build a following. Pinterest is hot, so a lot of people are hoping its success rubs off on them, but if you don't see a four-fold increase after one week on Pinterest, don't abandon in discouragement.

Look at the Pinterest story itself: it slowly built a solid user base until—after two years—reaching an explosion point. There are overnight success stories on Pinterest, but there are also many solid, steadily growing companies that, in our humble opinion, are more likely to stick around longer.

Finding the Right Person for the Job

Although curating Pinterest boards could be a full-time job, it's probably not cost-effective to make it one. When Christine was curating boards for a few clients, she promised them six to eight pins an hour, which translated into well-researched, representative pins. After your plan is in place and your initial boards are set up, a curator should expect to spend about an hour a day on Pinterest to make it an effective part of your online marketing strategy.

Who curates your Pinterest boards depends on the size of your company and your resources. If you're a one-person show, more than likely you curate your boards yourself. If you work in a small company with 10 or fewer employees, 1 or 2 people may have curating responsibilities. In larger companies, it might make sense to have a curator in each department to represent your different product lines or service offerings.

Pinterest is about aesthetics, so the person who curates your boards could be in the graphic design department as opposed to public relations or marketing. The person who maintains your Facebook status updates and Tweets on a daily basis might not be the right person for the Pinterest curator position.

The ultimate curator has a mix of experience as a search-engine technologist, marketing expert, and aesthete. In absence of the Pinterest superhero, the curator should think and act like a publisher and meet the following requirements:

- Be able to visually reflect the company image
- Understand the business, marketing, and Pinterest goals
- Be internet savvy—remember the curator has to both pin company information and source outside pins
- Be collaborative and responsive, able to spot trends

Outsourcing Options

Your best curator could be outside your company. Because pinning is such a new task, some companies are hiring external curators to pin on their behalf. You can contract an experienced pinner to curate your boards, much like you would hire a writer to work on brochure copy or blogs. You can find such curators by searching Pinterest itself for top pinners who have a large following and an aesthetic that matches your company's aesthetic.

You could also search for guest pinners to collaborate with you. At first, this may seem mercenary. But keep in mind that followers are very loyal, and if a pinner begins pinning things that aren't in keeping with their known aesthetic, followers might drop off. That's why you want to identify a curator who has an aesthetic that matches yours.

VERY PINTERESTING!

According to the 2012 Edelman Trust Barometer, people trust people who they see most like themselves in various aspects—physical, socioeconomic standing, education, familial status, and so on. They also need to hear something three to five times before they believe it.

Guest curators should be clear that they're pinning on behalf of your company. Transparency is a key element of Pinterest marketing. The upside to this scenario is that you accrue the curator's following right from the get-go, and top pinners already have sources for pins outside your company.

Brand Advocates

Brand advocates talk about your products or services in various social media outlets, as well as their personal blogs or *vlogs*.

DEFINITION

Similar to written blogs, **vlogs** are video blogs posted and promoted using the same marketing methods as a text blog. They're often posted to YouTube or Vimeo, too, which broadens the audience reach beyond blog subscribers.

Statistically, brand advocates mention a product or service nine times in a year. Brand advocates won't curate your boards on a regular basis, but they are adjunct voices in your online presence. It's your responsibility to keep your brand advocates up to date on your new products and services, and it's at their discretion to mention you or not.

Merging Your Communities

Pinterest will be a part of your social media marketing efforts. The built-in Facebook and Twitter links make it easy to announce any pins or boards you create automatically on Facebook and Twitter. But don't just pin and share anything and everything. Consider your options wisely because you want to create a constant presence, but you don't want to be annoyingly present. The number-one reason people unsubscribe to email newsletters, Facebook pages, or Twitter feeds is receiving too many communications too frequently.

Test the waters to determine how much is enough and how much can be too much. Better yet, offer your subscribers and followers a frequency option so that those who love you can hear from you every day or every week, and others can choose a once-a-month option. This keeps you in touch with your customers but also shows you respect their time. (We explore the technical aspects of this topic in depth in Chapter 9.)

Whether you've been using social media to market your products and services for a long time or you're new to the game, consider adopting a social media policy for your company. You can find an example, which you may modify or use (with the appropriate attribution) at ericschwartzman.com/pr/schwartzman/social-media-policy-template.aspx. The social media policy offers rules and guidelines for your company and employees about the interaction of personal social media engagement and company representation.

The Least You Need to Know

- Clearly define your Pinterest goals, and make them cohesive with your business objectives.
- Define your ideal customer in as much detail as possible; consider not only gender, age, and socioeconomic standing but also problems, desires, and interests.
- Use the Pinterest Marketing Diamond to lay out the structure and focus of your boards and pins.

- Create a task-oriented plan for meeting each goal using a tool such as mind mapping or an outline.
- Identify the person who will curate your Pinterest boards, as well as potential influencers and brand advocates.

Pinterest and Your Marketing Strategy

In This Chapter

- Sharing your brand voice
- Copywriting for your brand on Pinterest
- Making your brand a trusted source
- Introducing your audience to your company culture
- Creating content around popular Pinterest topics

By now, you might be coming to the realization that marketing on Pinterest is very different from marketing on other social media platforms like Facebook and Twitter. The key to marketing on Pinterest lies within your company's ability to tell a visually compelling "story" in order to engage your followers and potential customers on a more visceral level.

As we continue to dive into some of the more substantive ideas behind marketing your brand on Pinterest, this is a good time to take a pause and think about what Pinterest is. Breaking it down into elevator pitch form, Pinterest is a visual way of showcasing everything you love and find inspiring on the internet. As we take you through Chapter 6, be sure to keep in mind this very basic Pinterest concept.

Projecting Your Brand Voice onto Pinterest

On Pinterest, your *brand voice* is a visual one. Keeping in mind what the Pinterest platform is used for, it's obvious why those individuals and brands that are able to communicate visually stunning content to their followers are some of the more successful Pinterest users. Therefore, your ultimate goal on Pinterest is to create an account with a strong visual impact consistent with your brand voice across other marketing and advertising assets such as websites, brochures, Facebook, and so on. Many companies miss the mark and have different voices for each asset, causing a bit of brand confusion.

DEFINITION

Your **brand voice** is the cohesive and coherent narrative that tells your brand's story throughout all the content you put forth.

If it helps, think of Pinterest like you would a site like Flickr. Typically, on Flickr, the most popular users are those with beautiful, striking, and top-quality images. After all, nobody wants to spend their time looking through unattractive photos. With this concept in mind, be sure you always project the most visually appealing brand voice onto Pinterest.

Let's look at some great examples of brands that are projecting a strong "visual voice" on Pinterest.

New York–based shoe company Le Bunny Bleu "specializes in Romantic & Vintage Style women's flat shoes that include: Ballet Flats, Slip Ons, Oxfords, Sandals, Fashion Sneakers, Rain Boots and Wool Boots." Keeping in mind the company's theme of "romantic vintage," Le Bunny Bleu has cleverly opted to communicate their brand voice through stylish and elegant vintage fashion photography images and romantic interior spaces.

Le Bunny Bleu's Pinterest boards cover a range of topics
that illustrate their unique brand voice.

Thinking about the precious nature of their shoe designs and the company's trademark bunny, Le Bunny Bleu has taken its brand voice on Pinterest a few steps further by pinning images of sweet dessert recipes and adorable images of bunnies among a series of other brand-appropriate board topics. While Le Bunny Bleu has a limited number of boards (in comparison to others), its brand voice on Pinterest communicates a distinct message one would easily identify as sweet, feminine, cute, romantic, and vintage.

Here's another. Enjoy Events, a small wedding and event-planning business located in Northern California, prides itself on bringing a great deal of personal style to any happy occasion. Its bright and cheery style is communicated well through the visual brand voice it projects on its Pinterest account. From colorful inspiration boards to wedding décor ideas, the bright and colorful nature of its Pinterest content makes it apparent that this event planning duo knows how to bring a distinct point of view through its stylized work.

Enjoy Events' boards include imagery that clearly illustrates their bright and imaginative approach to weddings.

Furniture and home décor brand West Elm has consistently projected one of the strongest brand voices on Pinterest. West Elm, which "designs clean, simple products for modern living," clearly communicates its brand love for beautiful, high design. West Elm enjoys projecting its brand voice through imagery that covers a range of different decorating styles and approaches. After all, the company's "clean, simple products" can work well in a variety of different décor themes. But where West Elm really begins to create a visual voice that stands out from the crowd is through its supplementary images around color and pattern themes.

PIN TIP

When in the process of working out your brand's distinct Pinterest point of view, keep in mind key words that describe your company. Oftentimes, these key word adjectives—like Le Bunny Bleu's "romantic, vintage" style—make your visual voice very apparent.

West Elm doesn't stop at boards that revolve around furniture and décor objects; they also focus on colors, patterns, and design styles.

Writing Pinteresting Copy

While it's true that a picture speaks a thousand words, in Pinterest's case, it never hurts to add a few more. In fact, if the words are well thought out and delivered in the right tone, they enhance the beautiful images you pin. In many cases, Pinteresting copy can help push that prospective product buyer over the edge by adding a last bit of irresistible information.

The copy, or text, you write on your company's pins are just as important as the copy on your company's website, and should be carefully thought about and just as well executed. When you're communicating via the internet, it's crucial to utilize each and every opportunity you have to sell your services and/or products. Typically, you only have two opportunities: the images you put forth, and the copy that accompanies those images. If you were to ignore the second opportunity you have to communicate to your audience by neglecting to include copy on your pins, you sell your brand, and your pins, short. And what successful business wants to do that?

Tips for Creating Quality Copy

When Christine was in the process of launching her first ecommerce business, she decided to focus her limited funds and time on two crucial elements of her online retail store: the product photography and the website copy. As she anticipated, allocating a lot of her efforts and resources to those two components proved to be a wise decision.

Because she feels so strongly about the importance of quality copy, she thought she would take the opportunity to provide a few of her best tips here. Not only should you keep these ideas in mind when writing your Pinterest copy, but you can also apply them to your existing website and other social media platforms to help take your business to the next level.

First up, know your target audience, and know them well. While this may sound basic, many companies neglect to consider who it is they're speaking to and therefore often miss the opportunity to connect with their potential customers on a more personal level.

Be sure to provide as much information as possible by being descriptive. Ordering products and services and inquiring about a business online isn't 100 percent comfortable for even the most frequent internet users. Alleviate some of the doubts around your products and/or services by providing as much descriptive information as possible.

Also, connect on an emotional level. Generally, the purchases we love the most are based on emotions and not necessarily on rationality. We see something we love, and it speaks to a part of us that we often don't even know exists. Sometimes we want without even knowing why, but we do know that we love it, desire it, and *need* it. Tap into these feelings when creating your copy by painting a complete and alluring picture.

Create the lifestyle around your products and/or services by providing suggestions for how you or your products can fit into your customer's life. There are many instances in which we see a product, and love that product, but aren't ready to commit because we can't find the answer to that final (and most important) question: *How will I use this product?* Answer the question for your potential customers by suggesting ways they can make the most of their purchase. For example, if you're in fashion retail, provide style tips like "Wear these shoes with your favorite flare leg or skinny jeans. Either way, they'll look perfect!"

VERY PINTERESTING!

Sometimes, even with the best tips and advice possible, copywriting doesn't come easily. This doesn't mean you should give up on great copy. Websites like Copyblogger.com provide endless amounts of resources to help you along on your copywriting adventure!

Now that we know some of the rules around writing great copy, let's discuss how to create captivating copy on your company's pins. Generally, there are three types of pins you'll be pinning onto your company's Pinterest account: product pins, lifestyle pins, and tutorial pins. In the following sections, we describe each one and share some Pinteresting copy tips for each, plus great examples to help you paint the full picture.

Writing Pinteresting Copy for Product Pins

Product pins are those pins that feature a single product that links back to your or an ecommerce website. Typically, these pins can be identified by the price tag on the pin. (We discuss the importance of pricing your product pins further in Chapter 9.)

When creating Pinteresting copy for product pins, you may be tempted to simply copy and paste the product description that already exists from your website onto your pin. Convenient as that may be, we advise against it.

Think of your product on Pinterest as serving the same function a sandwich board would serve outside a restaurant or retail store. The copy on your product pin should excite and entice Pinterest users to click through the pin to find out more and eventually purchase that product. On a product pin, don't be concerned with product spec information and anything too detailed. Instead, focus on painting that alluring picture.

Let's look at an example:

This product pin could easily stand on its own because the purse is eye-catching and has been photographed well. However, Christine decided to take this pin above and beyond by adding additional information to help seal the deal for prospective buyers:

> Vieta Pink Zamora Sunset Purse. A rainbow of colors in a Southwestern print. This purse has so much happening on its own that I would style it down with a simple v-neck t-shirt and jeans.

For search purposes, she started out with the name of the designer (Vieta) and the name of the product (Pink Zamora Sunset Purse). We discuss search terms of pins on Chapter 9. For now, focus on the copy that follows the product name.

With the product copy, Christine was able to paint the full picture by highlighting what was special about this purse (i.e., the rainbow of colors in a Southwestern print) and give the purse some lifestyle context with how-to style information (i.e., This purse has so much happening on its own that I would style it down with a simple V-neck T-shirt and jeans.) And as you may or may not be able to see from the comments that followed, her followers were thankful for the "awesome styling suggestion," and a few of them shared their purchasing joy with comments like "I just bought this. I'm so excited. Thank you!"

We consider this an extremely successful product pin. Without the addition of Christine's additional copy, chances are this particular pin may have gotten lost in the mix.

PIN TIP

Don't be afraid to offer product advice and speak with authority! Remember, you know your own products better than anyone else, so feel free to give your product a strong endorsement and some great recommended uses. Your followers will thank you!

Writing Pinteresting Copy for Lifestyle Pins

Lifestyle pins are those pins that don't feature a specific product, but instead showcase a variety of photographs whose purpose is to enhance a brand's Pinterest voice. Lifestyle pins can include, but are not limited to, photos of inspiring interiors, vacation destinations, city streets, textile prints, etc. These types of lifestyle pins are very important in helping illustrate the full story around your brand, and they help your customers and/or clients connect with every aspect of what it is you're selling.

When creating Pinteresting copy for lifestyle pins, keep in mind the natural story the images on these pins already tell. Your job is to make them that much more tangible in order to tap into the viewers' feelings and experience of that pin.

For example, Calypso St. Barth is a fashion retail company that specializes in high-end resort-wear clothing, accessories, and home décor products. To illustrate their brand lifestyle and draw their new and existing customers into the Calypso St. Barth world, they started a lovely Pinterest board titled "Getaway In Style."

This is a great example of Pinteresting copy on a lifestyle pin:

> There is something so calming about the simplicity of the sand, ocean, and a beach fence directing you straight towards the water...

On its own, the photograph is beautiful and serene with soft colors reminiscent of the natural and pastel hues found in Calypso St. Barth's clothing and accessories. But the storylike quality of the copy on this pin helps transport the viewer to a tranquil spot on the beach where he may just dream of lying in a Calypso St. Barth swimsuit. At the very least, Calypso's followers are able to get a strong visual sense of what living the Calypso St. Barth life looks like. And it's a lovely life to want to aspire to!

Writing Pinteresting Copy for Tutorial Pins

Tutorial pins are any pins that link to DIY tutorials, recipes, downloadable projects, or instructional web posts and articles of any kind. Tutorial pins are some of the most popular pins on Pinterest and can help enhance your brand in several different ways. (We discuss those later in this chapter.)

Just by the nature of these types of pins, anyone who clicks through is led to a very text-heavy web post full of instructions for the tasty treat or DIY project pictured. On these pins, therefore, it's important for your copy to get your followers excited about the project pictured.

Here's a good example:

This pin is a photograph of a summer cocktail drink linking to a recipe and how-to instructions. Like the other examples shown in this chapter, this very attractive drink photograph is a fantastic pin on its own, but don't stop there, particularly on these types of food pins where it may not be clear that the pin links over to the how-to.

Here's the copy:

> Champagne, lemon sorbet and mint cocktail. Sounds like the BEST slushy summer cocktail ever! I'll definitely be serving this to my house guests as soon as the weather heats up. I may also try substituting the lemon sorbet for watermelon. (recipe)

This copy is effective for a few reasons. When writing copy for a tutorial pin, it's always good to let your followers and fellow pinners know what they're looking at right away by introducing it with a title. In this case the title is "Champagne, lemon sorbet and mint cocktail." Christine likes to follow these pin titles with a bit of enthusiasm over her discovery. Being genuine is always important. In this case, she was quite excited to come across this delicious drink recipe and will most definitely be serving these to her summer guests.

And if it's possible, feel free to propose your own spin on the tutorial you're sharing. In this example, Christine suggested substituting the lemon sorbet with watermelon. Oftentimes, this last bit helps start a conversation around your pin. And starting conversations is always a good thing! Your own take on a tutorial just might encourage others to share their own.

PIN TIP

Although Pinterest enables you to write quite a bit of copy on your pins, refrain from going overboard. Packing as much information as you can into a concise and engaging pin description is always the most effective route to take. Remember, quality over quantity!

Becoming a Go-To Source for Trusted Information

A major key to building a stellar reputation for your business and your Pinterest following is your ability to become a go-to source for trusted information. Outside Pinterest, if your customers and clients know they can rely on your company to provide them with the most reliable information or the best selection of products, your business becomes their go-to source time and time again. And if they're particularly fond of what you put out, they're likely to refer you to others.

The same holds true for successful brands on Pinterest. When a brand on Pinterest is able to generate high-quality and engaging pins day after day, Pinterest users start to realize they can rely on you to keep them entertained with the content you put forth. And not just entertained, but *informed* on some of the latest or coolest finds available.

And just like happy clients and customers will begin to recommend your business offline, your Pinterest followers will start to "recommend" you to their followers by repinning your content, bringing that many more interested eyes over to what you do.

How can you become a trusted and go-to source of information on Pinterest? The following helpful tips should send you well on your way:

First and foremost, decide what type of information makes sense for your brand to put forth. For example, if you're a brand that focuses around products for babies, you could easily become a go-to source for information relating to the best parenting books. If your brand focuses on pets, you can become a go-to resource for the best dog parks in America. Be sure that whatever topic you become an "expert" in is relevant to your brand.

Be sure to show off your industry knowledge. Pinterest is the perfect place to let everyone know how informed you are about the industry you work within and represent. Don't shy away from speaking with authority through your copy and becoming a thought leader through your pins.

The success your brand has on Pinterest relies heavily on your brand's ability to organize content around a theme. In the process of becoming a go-to source of trusted information, be sure to focus time and effort in curating relevant information within the topic you're an expert in. High-quality and informative pins stand a great chance at being repinned over and over again.

Fashion director of *Marie Claire Magazine* and *Project Runway* judge Nina Garcia knows how to be a trusted source of go-to information both on and off Pinterest. On Pinterest, Nina sets a strong example by constantly creating new boards to stay on top of fast-changing seasonal fashion trends. Nina Garcia's followers know they can rely on her pins to keep them up to date on everything that's fresh and new in fashion.

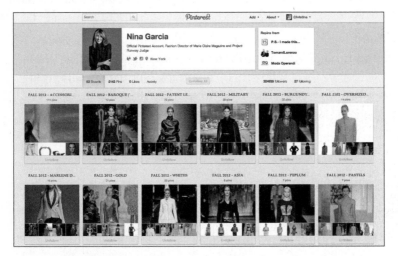

Season after season, fashion editor Nina Garcia keeps her Pinterest followers up to date on the latest trends.

PIN TIP

Remember that pin consistency is always important, particularly when building your brand's reputation as a go-to source. Think of your brand's Pinterest account as a news source, and be sure to send out daily tidbits of information.

Presenting Your Company and Going Behind the Scenes

One of the wonderful things social media has enabled brands to do over the past decade is give fans a sneak peek into the daily ins and outs of their operations. In some cases, you even have social media employees stepping out in front of some brands and sharing their daily duties as an ambassador of that brand. Whether it's office antics, peeks at new product arrivals, or company parties and events, more and more brands are helping us get excited about more than the products or services they provide. They're giving us the opportunity to fall in love with their company culture as well.

Most brands putting forth the effort to engage with their customers and clients in this new and exciting way either have or are in the process of figuring out how to do this effectively on Facebook and Twitter. But social media marketing on Pinterest requires a much different approach. Remember, the vast majority of your interaction on Pinterest is done visually. Brands that are able to provide their audience with visually exciting behind-the-scenes content have a successful presence on Pinterest.

The *Today* show does a superb job of giving Pinterest users a peek into the behind-the-scenes hijinks that happen on and off set, in between takes, and after the cameras stop rolling. Their clever and hilarious Pinterest board called "Anchor Antics" is full of candid snapshots of *Today* anchors having fun on the job. The pinned images exude personality, and many fans feel that much more connected to the *Today* anchors because of it. How can you not adore anchor Lester Holt after seeing a photo of him with his newly adopted rescue pup, Maddie?

Going behind the scenes with your brand is a relatively new concept, and its purpose might not be so obvious to everyone. Just in case you're not entirely sold on how and why this can be an effective marketing approach, following are some reasons that might help you make sense of this behind-the-scenes social media strategy.

Today's *"Anchor Antics" board is full of smile-inducing
images that engage followers in a meaningful way.*

For most people, personalities are easier to engage with than
brands. So when you're able to infuse your brand with personalities,
customers and clients begin to feel attached to the content your
brand is putting out on a more personal level.

Building more intimate relationships with your customers and clients
helps turn fans into *brand advocates*. Brand advocates are powerful
in that they serve as a free sales force for your brand by spreading
positive information about you by word of mouth and across social
media platforms. In the case of Pinterest, these are the individuals
who pin and repin content from your website and Pinterest account
on a frequent basis.

DEFINITION

A **brand advocate** is an individual who is a fan of a brand to the extent
that he feels a sense of ownership over seeing that brand succeed. This
person is a volunteer marketer who uses his time to promote the brand
he loves without receiving payment to do so.

Behind-the-scenes glimpses can also act as "teasers" for your audience. Back when Christine owned a retail business, she used to enjoy sharing images of her opening shipment boxes of cool new products, and her customers were always anxious to see what products were coming just around the corner. Going behind the scenes is a great way of generating excitement!

Recently Christine had the good fortune of following a fantastic brand mentioned earlier in this chapter, Calypso St. Barth, on an exciting trip to the island of St. Barts. Her job was to accompany the Calypso team on an island photo shoot for their 2012 summer look book and document the shoot on Pinterest in a first-time-ever "live pinning event." By utilizing the Pinterest application on her iPhone, Christine was able to snap photos of Calypso's photo shoot, products, team, and St. Barts scenery, and upload those photos onto a collaborative "Island Photoshoot" board in real time. Because the Island Photoshoot board was a collaborative board between Calypso St. Barth and Christine, both her followers and theirs were able to share in this experience.

This type of behind-the-scenes Pinterest collaboration between a *power pinner* and a brand had never been tested before, and Christine admits she was quite nervous about how the event and partnership would be received. In order to maintain as much consistency as possible between the new content she was pinning with the type of content she usually pins, Christine was sure to snap images that were full of vibrant colors and stylized fashion shots. This type of content also worked well with Calypso's existing content and complemented the lifestyle it was already communicating through its pins.

DEFINITION

A **power pinner** is a Pinterest user who has accumulated an extremely large following and whose pins and repins have a significant amount of influence on Pinterest and elsewhere.

Overall, it was a very successful power pinner and brand collaborative Pinterest event, and all followers were overwhelmingly excited about the content being pinned. In fact, several of the stylized product shots led to sales and a tremendous amount of excitement over Calypso St. Barth's collection. Enabling followers to view products in a lifestyle context through a behind-the-scenes campaign proved to be a smart marketing approach.

PIN TIP

When uploading photos you've taken to Pinterest, consider using photo filters through photo applications, or services like Instagram, to give your photos a unique and pinworthy quality. Enhancing photo colors helps them pop that much more on Pinterest.

Making Pinterest "Hot Topics" Work for Your Brand

Pinterest "hot topics" are the categories on Pinterest that are currently most popular. For purposes of marketing on Pinterest and appealing to the Pinterest demographic, it's a good idea to incorporate some of these hot-topic categories into the content you pin.

However, that doesn't mean you should pin DIY projects on your company's Pinterest account if this topic is in no way brand appropriate. Appearing disingenuous on Pinterest or any other social media platform just to fit in is never a good idea.

Instead, focus on the hot-topic categories that are not only relevant, but help enhance your brand. Here are some of the hot topics:

- Food and Drink
- DIY and Crafts
- Architecture and Home Decor
- Adorable Animals
- Inspirational Quotes
- Fashion and Beauty
- Products

Creating Pinterest boards for your company's account that incorporate all these hot topics is impossible. But almost every brand can find relevance in at least one of these hot-topic boards. You'll be excited to know that sometimes all it takes is a bit of creativity to make a hot-topic board work for you.

For example, if you represent a business within the tech industry, you may be looking at these popular topics and scratching your head. Let's look at some ways to make a few of the hot-topic categories work for a challenging tech-focused brand:

Food and Drink. Everyone eats, right? Even tech engineers who sit behind a computer most of the day. Make Food and Drink work for your company by sharing some of your office's favorite takeout locations and after-work pubs. This could be an exciting go-to reference board for other businesses and customers in your neighborhood.

Architecture and Home Decor. More and more tech and startup offices are starting to create some of the coolest and most interesting office spaces around. Use your design-savvy tech sense to create a board featuring your favorite well-designed startup office spaces.

Products. Everyone involved in the tech industry loves and lives by their gadgets. Showcase your office's favorite tech gear in a product board featuring the best gadgets available. No doubt, someone in the office owns or has used some of the products you feature on this board. Product reviews can make some of the most interesting and effective Pinterest copy, so be sure you include a short review with your pin.

> **MARKETING MIX-UP**
>
> Don't force a hot-topic board to work for your brand if it's impossible. The last thing you want to do is pin content that's irrelevant to your brand and confusing to your audience.

Let's come back to a brand we mentioned earlier in this chapter, Le Bunny Bleu, as an example of a shoe brand that made a seemingly irrelevant hot-topic board work for it. While it may have seemed obvious for a brand that has "bunny" in its name to create a board full of cute photos of bunnies, we still have to hand it to Le Bunny Bleu for its creativity. You have to admire a brand that focuses on shoes that can make an adorable animal hot-topic board work in such a seamless and brand-relevant way.

Shoe company Le Bunny Bleu created an adorable and irresistible board featuring cute bunnies, making a Pinterest hot topic work for the brand.

Just because it seems obvious in hindsight, it isn't always in the moment. So be sure you're paying attention and staying creative.

The Least You Need to Know

- Your brand voice on Pinterest is a visual one. Make your voice louder than the rest by pinning visually stunning content.
- High-quality copy always helps enhance even the most beautiful image.
- In general, there are three types of pins you'll use for your business—product pins, lifestyle pins, and tutorial pins—and the copy for each serves a different function.
- Don't be afraid to speak with authority when pinning content within your industry; becoming a go-to source of trusted information requires that you know well what you pin.
- Giving your Pinterest followers a behind-the-scenes glimpse into your company culture helps build fans and excite brand advocates.
- Most brands can make hot-topic boards work for them; the key is to get creative when thinking about your business in relation to popular Pinterest topics.

Brainstorming Boards for Your Brand Narrative

In This Chapter

- Your brand presented visually
- Creating board topics for your target audience
- Writing board titles to capture your audience
- Building boards that target a specific topic
- Organizing your boards

Brands have been visually communicating with people for hundreds of years through print campaigns. And since the beginning, the most effective and memorable visual campaigns have been those that feature a combination of striking photos, gorgeous typography, and smart graphics. Whether you describe yourself as "visual" or not, there's no denying the power of a strong image.

Thinking about what Pinterest enables brands to achieve visually, it's no wonder the site is already making a significant impact for businesses that have figured out how to use Pinterest to their advantage by playing to their visual strengths. In this chapter, we show you how to create Pinterest boards that effectively tell your *brand narrative* in a compelling way.

Visually Telling the Story of Your Brand

One of the most important boards, or series of boards, your brand should create on Pinterest are those that communicate the story of your company. These types of brand storyboards are incredibly compelling to those who follow your brand, and they're full of the type of information that turns these followers into true fans. The more we know about the story and history of a brand, the more inclined we are to identify with it and connect with the journey that brand has been on.

DEFINITION

A **brand narrative** includes the stories, messages, and experiences that tell the past and current history of a brand.

For example, Christine has always liked and appreciated the quality of the products The North Face and Patagonia have produced, although the sticker shock of the majority of their active wear has often kept her from making purchases.

In 2010, a documentary titled *180° South* traced the journey to Patagonia, Argentina, of The North Face founder Douglas Tompkins and his friend, Patagonia founder Yvon Chouinard. This monumental trip would later inspire their multimillion-dollar companies and also leave them with a strong sense of wanting to protect this region of the planet. Today, both founders have used their fortunes to protect more than 2 million acres of precious land throughout South America. Since learning about the history of The North Face and Patagonia, Christine has allowed herself to splurge on their products, knowing that a portion of what she's spending is going toward these preservation efforts.

Christine's personal experience with knowing the history of The North Face and Patagonia is a prime example of why telling your brand narrative can be a valuable marketing tactic and a great way of cultivating a loyal customer base. Storytellers make the best product sellers.

So now that you know why telling your brand narrative is so very important, let's go over two unique ways to communicate your brand's history on Pinterest.

Creating a Storyboard

Back in the very early days of Pinterest, San Francisco–based blogger Victoria Smith of sfgirlbybay.com co-created a Pinterest event with Pinterest co-founder Ben Silbermann called "Pin It Forward." This event was one of the first efforts made to help spread the word about the new site and build a network of first Pinterest users. Every day, a handful of different bloggers were asked to create a board based on the subject of what "home" meant to them. Over the course of two months, hundreds of bloggers created boards around this topic.

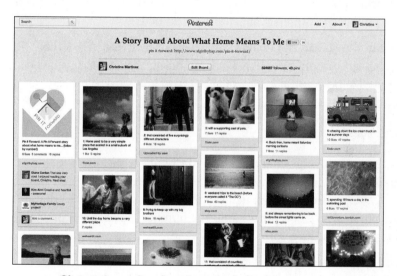

Christine's storyboard on the topic of what home means to her created for the "Pin It Forward" Pinterest event.

Being one of the first bloggers to launch this "Pin It Forward" event with Victoria Smith, and being a natural storyteller, Christine decided to communicate what "home" meant to her by creating a storyboard with numbers to provide direction on how to read her story. The concept was simple: she wanted to tell her own story using a series of photos that complemented the story copy she wrote on those pins. That way, the story would appear in a comic book–like fashion, sans comedy. While the concept was simple, executing it took a bit of time and thought. Here's how she did it:

With a pen and paper (remember those archaic tools?), she wrote out the story she wanted to tell and then broke up the story into a series of sentences that would be written on each pin.

She then spent several hours scouring the internet for high-quality images that would accompany the text of her story. She used keywords from sentences in her story in her search—for example, *college, Los Angeles, party, Chihuahua.*

Christine created a bookmark folder on her computer with the links to the images she found and numbered them in the "bookmark title" in order to keep track of which story sentence they corresponded to. Keeping everything organized proved to be key.

When she had all the images she needed, Christine began the storyboard pinning process. Understanding that the first pins on a board appear at the *bottom* of that board and work their way up, Christine essentially told her story backward, from the end of the story, or last pin, to the beginning, or first pin. That way, it read correctly on the finished board.

Because of the uneven grid nature of Pinterest, she also added numbers onto each pin to help her followers read the story more easily. Also, because comments added to pins after the fact change the physical size of a pin, adding the numbers to each pin proved to be very helpful over time.

Just like every individual, every brand has a history and a story to tell. So a storyboard like this is an incredibly creative way to create a visual storyboard for your brand's history. Although Christine made this board nearly two years ago, she still receives comments from Pinterest users who appreciate the unique way she utilized a Pinterest board.

This pin contains no comments and appears as a "normal" size pin.

This pin contains several comments and has now taken on a much longer shape. If not for the numbers added, a long pin like this may make a storyboard difficult to read.

Have fun, get creative, and share your brand history through a Pinterest storyboard!

Using Archived Information to Tell Your Brand Story

If storyboarding your brand's history is an endeavor you'd rather not tackle, there are plenty of other creative ways to visually communicate your brand's history on Pinterest. Let's look at another fantastic approach that might just get your wheels turning.

TIME Magazine's *Pinterest board features popular magazine covers from past issues.*

TIME Magazine is a brand with an impressive and long history. Taking advantage of their archives of decades' worth of *TIME Magazine* imagery, *TIME* decided to share some of its brand history on a board titled "Vintage TIME Covers" to showcase "TIME's most notable covers throughout its 89-year-old history." This fascinating Pinterest board evokes feelings of nostalgia and a greater appreciation for the groundbreaking stories and events *TIME Magazine* has covered over nearly nine decades.

Your company might not have this type of history or imagery archives to draw from, but that doesn't mean you have to shy away from creating historic boards like *TIME*'s. Again, give it some solid thought and then really get creative.

For example, Christine's ecommerce store had a brief, four-year history. But during that time, she had a series of her own personal historic moments that were important to her brand. She could have created a history board and included images of the first shipment she sent out, clips of press she received, and photos from buying trips abroad.

Remember, if it's interesting to you, chances are it's interesting to the people who admire your brand, too.

Profiling Customers to Create Board Topics

Recently, Christine has started to consult with a range of businesses, both large and small, that would like to start using Pinterest but don't know where to begin. Most of the companies she works with start a board or two showing their products but then feel a bit lost with where to go from there. If this is how you feel, don't worry. You're certainly not alone.

The process of building a brand's Pinterest account is quite similar to the process of creating a brand in the first place. You have to know your desired customer or client well in order to put out the information or products that person will get excited about. The same is true on Pinterest. Knowing your existing and desired customers well helps you make informed decisions on what type of visual content you need to pin to draw in your new customers—and just as importantly, keep your current customers engaged.

The first step in building content on your Pinterest account is creating your Pinterest boards. Christine likes to recommend that businesses start with about 10 boards. When she sits down to brainstorm with brands about what these first 10 Pinterest boards should be, she likes to start by profiling that business's ideal customer or client. It's worth repeating: you need to know your existing and desired customers well in order to make informed decisions on what type of visual content to put forth.

Let's go through the steps of profiling your ideal customer: remember those little brainstorming clouds we were taught to make in school? Create one of those! At the center, make up the name, gender, and age of your ideal customer.

Begin to create the story of that ideal customer by asking yourself some very basic questions about the person you're profiling. For example, does this person prefer to read books or magazines? If the answer is books, what kinds of books? What does this person do for fun? What are some of this person's favorite things to eat?

As you keep asking these types of questions about your ideal customer, you'll notice your brainstorming bubble is starting to branch out in several different directions. That's great! Keep going. It may seem like a silly task, but by doing this, you're creating the story of the type of person you want to attract.

After you've filled your page, read the full *customer profile* you've created. Does this sound like the person you want to work with? It should! Take a moment to congratulate yourself on profiling your ideal customer. This is valuable information that will help you create your brand's Pinterest boards.

 DEFINITION

A **customer profile** contains the likes, dislikes, personality traits, and characteristics that make up a brand's target customer.

Now let's translate the character traits you've come up with into interesting, engaging, and brand-relevant Pinterest boards. We'll use Nike to illustrate this process. You might imagine that a company like Nike, with thousands of different products for a wide range of sports and physical activities, would have no problem creating several boards around the products they offer. But as we're starting to understand with Pinterest, brands that are successfully marketing on this platform are going beyond their products and introducing Pinterest users to the entire *lifestyle* around their brand. That's where these types of customer profiles are going to come in handy.

Based on the target Nike customer profile we generated earlier, let's say we've determined that Nike's target customer loves to live a healthy lifestyle that includes a well-balanced diet. In order to engage with the customer, we'd create a board full of beautifully photographed, light-fare dishes with recipes attached.

We've also determined that Nike's target customer is a self-motivated individual who feels connected with and inspired by inspirational quotes. For that customer, we'd create a board with graphic prints and posters that feature uplifting words of wisdom.

We've identified that the target Nike customer likes to watch sports-related movies. To keep that customer excited, we'd create a video board featuring trailers of some of the best sports films of all time.

PIN TIP

Don't forget you can upload videos to Pinterest. Many Pinterest users have yet to take advantage of the video pin feature. When you're creating captivating boards for your brand's Pinterest account, be sure to keep brand-relevant video boards in mind.

Creating Compelling Board Titles

Creating compelling board titles isn't necessarily essential to establishing a strong Pinterest presence, but it's essential to creating a cohesive and coherent brand tone. And ideally, the brand tone you have on Pinterest should be consistent with the brand tone you create off Pinterest—that is, on your website, blog, etc. Consistency across platforms is something all brands should practice as they dive into social media.

Compelling board titles are important because boards are the most prominent visual on a profile page. Board titles also make up the majority of the text Pinterest users see when they visit your company's Pinterest profile. So it's very possible to attract followers simply because your board titles grab their attention.

There are two different types of compelling board titles: clear and straightforward board titles, and whimsical and creative board titles. Clear and straightforward board titles are easy for Pinterest users to understand. There's no mystery around what type of pins will be found on those boards. The boards either cover a topic users are interested in, or not. Many Pinterest users prefer and appreciate this approach, and depending on your brand, this might be the right direction for you.

The second type of board title is compelling because it helps play on the fun and creative nature of the brand these boards represent. They are eye-catching and fit in well with Pinterest's entertaining nature.

Real Simple magazine has created a strong Pinterest presence with its beautiful and informative account that's perfectly reflective of its simple, eye-catching, and educational publication. With board titles like "Problem-Solving Products," "New Uses for Old Things," and "Best Slow-Cooker Recipes," *Real Simple*'s straightforward approach on Pinterest is clear and concise. And even though it doesn't use a lot of playful copy on Pinterest, its board titles are compelling because of the interesting topics they cover. *Real Simple*'s boards stand on their own without all the bells and whistles of humorous copy.

Real Simple *magazine's board titles are easy to understand and convey strong ideas.*

Fashion icon and stylist to the stars Rachel Zoe has recently created an account for her daily email newsletter, *The Zoe Report*. In a brand-appropriate fashion, *The Zoe Report*'s Pinterest boards reflect the more whimsical style of naming boards. With board titles like "Baubles & Bling," "It's In The Bag," and "Pretty In Prints," *The Zoe Report*'s full-of-fun approach is perfectly in line with the Pinterest fashionistas who adore Rachel Zoe. Her board titles are compelling because they speak directly to the young women who are attracted to lively fashion publications and having fun with fashion.

The Zoe Report*'s board titles are consistent with Rachel Zoe's general tone and figurative flair that appeals to her fans.*

Whichever board title approach you take, it's important to keep one very vital idea in mind: be sure Pinterest users understand what the contents of your boards are. Don't create board titles that are so clever or obscure for the sake of being different that you miss out on potential followers who are confused or who might even intentionally skip over your pins, assuming they're not interested.

For example, if you create a Pinterest board full of your favorite night creams, moisturizers, and sleeping masks and you title it "Night Owl," you might miss out on picking up other fans of nighttime essentials who don't realize "Night Owl" represents these products. Instead, opt for a board title that paints a clearer picture, like "Nourish Your Nighttime Face."

> **MARKETING MIX-UP**
>
> Creative board titles are fun, but when they don't include keywords to clearly describe their pin content, they end up getting lost in the search. Be sure to include keywords in your board titles.

Creating Boards with a Narrow Focus

As far as anyone can tell right now, the number of boards a user has doesn't seem to affect whether or not she is followed or her boards show up more prominently in search results. And as long as this trend continues, we say the more the merrier! Why not curate everything you love? As long as it's brand appropriate, that is. The one thing that's clear about boards is that the most effective and admired boards are narrow in focus. They have a clear direction and revolve around a very specific topic.

When you create boards that are narrow in focus, chances are you'll catch the attention of others who share in specific interest because these types of boards seem to resonate deeper with them. After all, as Pinterest users, we would all prefer to spend our time on the site looking at products and pictures that will enhance not only our user experience, but also our lives.

Just in case you aren't clear on what a narrow-focus board is, let's look at an example. A "Midcentury Furniture" board is a much more targeted board than one called simply "Furniture." Furniture is such a broad category, users who are looking to find midcentury furniture might skip right over it, or they might not find it at all, even if you're pinning a lot of midcentury furniture. Be sure the boards you create have a clear and specific topic. And be sure you title your boards accordingly.

One of Christine's most successful Pinterest boards is her "Words to Live By" board. On this board, she pins some of her favorite inspirational quotes she aspires to live her life by. Most users seem to find these quotes encouraging and uplifting. "Words to Live By" is a great example of a narrow-focus board because the content pinned on this board is very specific and doesn't deviate from the topic at hand. Pinterest users searching for inspirational quotes can find hundreds of them on Christine's focused "Words to Live By" board.

Christine's "Words to Live By" board is a prime example of a board with a narrow focus and features inspirational quotes around a positive theme.

The popular online wedding publication and boutique 100 Layer Cake has a range of wedding-related Pinterest boards. All these boards are visually fantastic, but the "Escort Cards" board jumps out as a prime example of a well-done narrow-focus board.

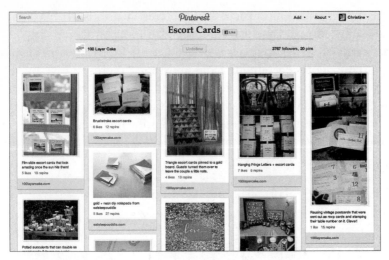

*This narrow-focus board by 100 Layer Cake dedicated to
escort cards is incredibly helpful for the bride looking for
escort card inspiration.*

It's easy to let yourself get a bit general with wedding-focused
Pinterest boards. In fact, most users who have boards about
weddings tend to include all aspects of a wedding, from dresses to
floral arrangements, on one board. 100 Layer Cake decided to take
the narrow-focus approach by creating an entire board specifically
dedicated to escort cards. For Pinterest users who are searching for
this very specific wedding component, this board is certainly an ideal
go-to source.

Customizing Your Board
Cover Photos

Just as board titles are important when viewing a user's Pinterest
profile page, so are the prominent board images. To give users
some additional visual control over their profile pages, Pinterest
has enabled users to decide which one of their pinned images best
represents a board they've created.

To change a board cover photo, hover your mouse over the board you want to change and click **Edit Board Cover**. Then just choose the image you want to appear as the board cover and drag it to where you want it. Click **Set Cover** when you're finished.

Use this opportunity to choose a beautiful image that will make your profile page just that much more exciting!

Arranging Your Boards

The ability to arrange your boards hasn't always been a feature available on Pinterest, and for some of us early users, it was incredibly exciting when this feature was added. Being able to arrange your Pinterest boards is such an important feature for brands specifically because it allows you to highlight and bring forth those boards that are either most current or most relevant. When you look at a profile page, the first five boards on your account are the ones with the best page real estate. Because these boards are front and center, it's important to be able to bring either your most current or your most popular boards to the top when you want or need to.

If you own a retail store, think of board arranging the same way you'd think about merchandising. You're always going to want to place your newest or most popular merchandise in the most visible area of your store. That's the same idea behind board arranging.

Marie Claire fashion editor and *Project Runway* judge Nina Garcia is someone who makes great use of this feature. Within the fashion industry, it's always crucial to be current. And a fashion editor at one of the biggest fashion publications in the world understands that better than most people. In order to keep her Pinterest account current with fashion trends, Garcia is mindful to place the most current fashion seasons at the top of her page, while fashion boards from seasons past move down to the bottom.

For fashion editor Nina Garcia, it's important to be on the forefront of trends. Arranging her boards from the most current on is important to her brand.

PIN TIP

Board arranging allows you to experiment with your account, and experimentation on Pinterest is great. Try changing the arrangement of your boards to find the most effective placement. If you find that giving a board prime page real estate at the top increases that board's following, be sure you rotate your boards periodically, giving all of them some time at the top.

The Least You Need to Know

- Visually communicating your company's history on Pinterest is a great way of engaging with your followers, and a perfect opportunity to share some interesting information about your company many users might not know.

- Getting creative with the ways in which you can visually tell your company's story is an effective way of standing out on Pinterest.

- It's vitally important to know the profile of your ideal customer or client well in order to make informed decisions about what types of content you should be putting out.
- Both clear and straightforward and whimsical and creative board titles attract users. Decide which is most appropriate for your brand.
- Boards with a narrow focus stand a much better chance of attracting other users who share that interest.
- Board arrangement gives you the opportunity to highlight your brand's most recent and relevant boards.

Making the Parts of a Pin Work for You

In This Chapter

- Showing your brand's best side
- Making your pins pop
- Getting the most out of pin space
- Engaging with other pinners
- Reclaiming lost links

Think of each of your pins as part of a message to your brand's followers—your existing and potential customers. Put together, your pins should tell a compelling story and lead your customers to make a decision, which could be as simple as deciding to learn more about your company, or as complete and complex as making a purchase. The decisions you want to encourage your followers to make are what drive the goals you established for your Pinterest presence, as discussed in Chapter 5.

Think about your ideal client and Pinterest goals you defined in Chapter 5. The pins you choose should support those goals and have the largest effect on your Pinterest presence. After all, your pins are what your followers come to see. In this chapter, we take you through the parts of a pin, give examples of effective pins, and show you how to get the most impact from each and every pin you make.

Putting Your Best Image Forward

The main part—although not the only part—of a pin is the image. We could describe a good pin with a plethora of adjectives, but sometimes a picture speaks a thousand words. You want that picture to speak about your brand, company, product, or service. You aren't limited to photos. You can pin infographics, sayings, drawings, places, books, movies, or pretty much anything you can think of, but as we write about later, whatever you pin should support your Pinterest goals.

In this section, we include a few images to give you an idea of what we consider a successful pin. We also suggest you look around Pinterest to get an idea of image style. Pretend you're one of your customers, and notice which images stand out and what works in images you like. Do you find you prefer single items or compositions? Does stark or warm lighting have a greater impact? Are you more inspired by color or black and white? Perhaps you're drawn to sayings. There's no one right answer, but as you look at pins through your ideal customer's eyes, you begin to get an idea of the types of images you'll want to pin.

Now let's look at some pins we find effective.

Fixing Photos clearly tells what it does with their boards. Its pins show before and after images that illustrate how it's made old photos look new. By using a variety of images, the company helps create customer identification. It also writes varied copy that not only describes how the photo was repaired but also includes something about customer service and prices. A URL is included in each description, too. We'd advise Fixing Photos to include a hashtag as well to increase its searchability. (More on hashtags in the "Using Hashtags in Your Pins" section later in this chapter.)

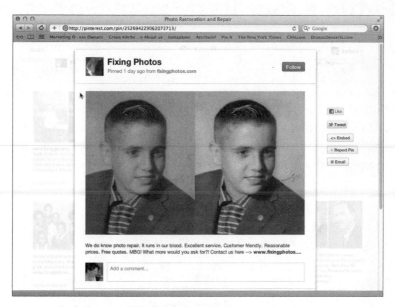

*Include as much information as you can in the pin
description, and vary the information from pin to pin.*
(© 2013 Fixing Photos)

PIN TIP

Even though your pin has a URL link embedded (you do include URLs
when you edit your pins, don't you?), you can add a URL in the pin
description—or better yet, use a shortened link such as bit.ly, which lets
you track the number of referrals that come from Pinterest. You even can
go a step further and use a specific bit.ly for each board to determine
which boards drive the most traffic to your website.

Domo is a cloud-based software solution that helps managers and
executives transform the way they run their businesses. Its pins are
colorful and informative, and they convey innovation and creativity,
echoing their product and service offering, which provides a new
type of business intelligence software. The infographic in the
following figure, one of several on a specific Domo Infographics
board, has their logo at the top and the bottom, and they've smartly

used the @ and # symbols to make it searchable (more about that later in this chapter).

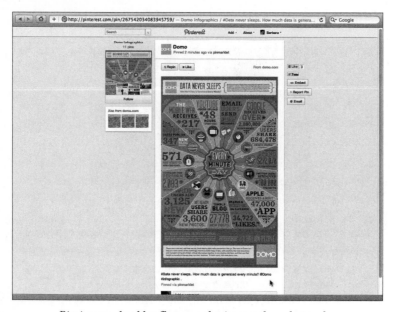

Pin images should reflect your business style and appeal to the audience you're trying to reach.
(© 2012 DOMO, Inc.)

We love Mark Shaw's creativity. He's an illustrator whose specialty is vintage cars. In this pin, he built a puzzle that definitely encourages repinning. He pinned one pin a day to a board, and by repinning the nine pins he posted, you can create a board that shows the final image. Then he made this pin that shows the final product, so it's the image of a board on a pin. His other boards show vintage autos and other auto- or retro-related pins.

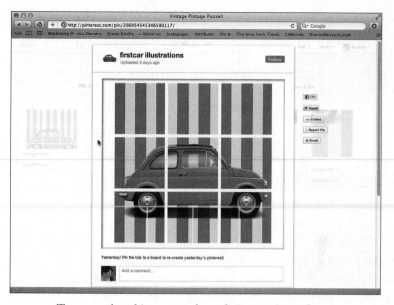

Turn your board into a puzzle, and pin one piece a day to keep followers coming back to see the next piece.
(© 2012 created by Firstcar Illustrations)

Encourage Repinning

Repinning spreads your image—and by default your brand—so aim to curate pins that attract repinning. The most successful pins are pretty, helpful, inspiring, or funny.

Granted, what's pretty can be subjective. For example, Barbara finds full-body tattoo pins disturbing, but no doubt there's a big audience for those pins. Helpful pins include graphic representations of how-to's, tutorials, recipes, and videos. Inspiring pins include great quotes or phrases, perhaps from someone in your company, and ideally presented in a graphically pleasing way. To house your funny pins, consider creating a just-for-fun board. However, pin cautiously so you won't offend any followers or put your company in a bad light.

We can't stress enough the importance creating *repinnable* pins and the unique opportunity repinning offers. The original URL stays with the pin whenever it's repinned, which means as your pin is repinned, the potential number of click-throughs to your URL grows. The value of a repin goes far beyond brand recognition to truly having an effect on increasing your customer base.

> **PIN TIP**
>
> Keep these tips in mind not only when pinning images, but also when you put images on your website or blog so that pinners can pin directly from there.

Repinning spreads the word about your products and services, but it's also a great tool to see what images are working for you. Go back through some of your pins that you think are most appealing and repinnable and see if they were repinned, or use an analytics service (as explained in Chapter 13) to see which of your pins have been repinned most frequently. This information can help you decide what to pin in the future. If one of your pins has been repinned 10, 1,000, or 15,000 times, you can attempt to re-create the look and feel of that pin to encourage more traffic to your brand's boards.

Keep It Relevant

You probably have a lot of great images, and it's understandable that you'd like to pin all of them. However, willy-nilly pinning isn't going to help you reach your Pinterest goals. Look through your images with a discerning eye, and choose those that are relevant to your overall business message and brand in the first place and also are relevant to the board where you pin them.

Relevance isn't limited to the content of the pin. It also includes the style. If you develop a board that has a color or seasonal theme, use pins that support that theme. If the board is meant to showcase products, pin a mix of catalog-style product shots and lifestyle shots that relate to the products. Companies like Kaufman Mercantile and

Williams-Sonoma do a great job of showing their own products and pinning images that convey the style their products solicit.

Relevance also pertains to the timeliness of a pin. Although you probably work on your Valentine's Day catalog sometime in August, you'll be better served to pin Valentine-themed images in late January, leaving enough time for the pins to show up in searches and appear at a time when people are ready to think about Valentine's Day.

Balance Content

Although it's acceptable to pin your own images—and you want to—a big part of the Pinterest etiquette and ethic is not to boast.

Aim to create a balance between your images and pins found elsewhere that correlate with your brand and represent the image you want to portray. The web is overflowing with fabulous images, but remember to avoid haphazard pinning. Pin content that enriches your brand, not something beautiful that competes with it.

PIN TIP

Resist the urge to pin anything and everything that catches your eye. Quality over quantity will win out every time!

Create a Dynamic Environment

Your followers return to your boards to see what's new, so you should pin on a regular basis to create a dynamic pin stream.

Ideally, your boards will have a variety of followers, and it's okay that not every one of your followers follows each of your boards. But this means you have to pay attention to distributing your pins across all your different boards rather than just loading up a few boards with the majority of your pins. We talk about timing your pins later in this chapter.

> **VERY PINTERESTING!**
>
> Mashable gives instructions for spreading one photo over nine pins,
> tic-tac-toe style, which can be an eye-catching site on your profile page.
> Learn how at mashable.com/2012/02/16/pinterest-hack-how-to.

Your Second Opportunity to Make a Pin Pop!

Under each pin, you can—and *should*—write a description. In fact, don't even think about pinning without a description. Pins without descriptions tend to get repinned less often, and you want your pins to be repinned.

What makes a good description? Many studies have been conducted to determine what works and what doesn't when writing Facebook posts and tweets, and some of the results can be applied to Pinterest descriptions as well. One we found interesting—if not surprising—is that descriptions of 80 characters or fewer have a higher engagement rate. If you have trouble keeping your tweets to 140 characters, 80 may seem impossible! However, remember you're writing a description that accompanies an image, and 80 characters *is* doable.

Descriptions should add value to your pin and, well, describe it. "Gotta have this!" is okay for a pin description when another user pins one of your products, but that's not something you, your brand, or your company should write. It's a comment, not a description.

Instead, think about what you want your followers to know about the pin. Answer the questions "where?" or "when?" the product or service in your pin would be used. Tell your followers what they could or should do with it.

On the other hand, don't use misleading pin descriptions. If your pin shows an image of a final product and the description reads "Do it yourself," the implication is that clicking through the link will lead to instructions on how to make the product shown in the pin. If you're selling kits to make the product, the description should read something like "Make your own doodah from our Doodah Kit, $25 on *yourwebsiteURL*.com."

Perhaps the most important thing to remember is to use at least one primary keyword to increase your *search engine optimization* (SEO). Pins are individually searchable, which makes keywords essential because when someone searches for a specific item or service—and you offer that item or service—you want your pins to appear in the search results. Keywords are also used by search engines, such as Google, Yahoo!, and Bing, to find matches when people conduct web searches.

DEFINITION

Search engine optimization is the process of identifying and using specific words, phrases, and images on your web pages, blogs, and pins that help you appear among the top results of web searches.

Let's look at a few more examples of good descriptions.

Amy Bowerman is the design force behind Plucking Daisies. She designed this Teacher Supplies Garden for a contest called the Scribble Challenge. The description aptly uses both the # (hashtag) symbol.

(Amy Bowerman, pluckingdaisies.com)

Rick Dohler puts his designs on Etsy and then pins them from Etsy to his Pinterest boards. He rightly put the dollar sign in the description and his company name, Dohler Designs. We like the close-up photo that shows details of the product.

(Rick Dohler, etsy.com/shop/DohlerDesigns?ref=sishop)

Renowned cooking supply manufacturer and retailer Williams-Sonoma puts up a recipe of the day (pinterest.com/williamssonoma/recipe-of-the-day). The # makes one ingredient of the recipe searchable, but the cleverness is that the image and recipe say "when you think of food, think Williams-Sonoma."

The description you write stays with the pin when it's repinned, so a good description literally goes a long way, and the less sales-y your description, the more likely it is to be repinned. Keep the *interest* in Pinterest when describing your pins. Write descriptions that convey the enthusiasm you have for your products and services. Describe them as you would to a good friend.

Barbara blogs about baking and pins photos of her efforts.
Her pin descriptions are compelling and inviting.

At the same time, you want followers to associate the image with your company or brand. Be sure your profile name and image, which should be your business name and logo, appear under the images you pin, and your pins appear on your followers' Pinterest home pages. You can, and should, put your company name in the description you write. A watermark on the image is another way to ensure the pin is recognized as something from your company.

PIN TIP

Be sure the pin is linked to your website so when viewers click on the enlarged image, they go directly to your website. Or better yet, link to the web page where the image came from. See Chapter 4 to learn more about links.

Maximizing Information on Your Pin

You can add symbols to your pin description that will cause your pin to appear in other places on Pinterest. By making the most of the information you write in the pin description, your pin is more searchable and therefore your brand's presence increases.

Pricing Your Pin

If you include a price with the $ (dollar) or £ (British pound) symbol, your pin is automatically included in the Gifts category on the main Pinterest page, as well as on your board. In today's economic climate, potential customers want an idea of how much your product or service costs before they take the next step to visit your website or contact you. Prices aren't limited to products, so think outside the box. If you offer a service, show an example of that service and include a price.

This is an effective tactic for online businesses that sell products but also for local businesses that offer services. For example, a hair salon could pin a beautiful coif and put a price in the description to indicate how much that style costs. A coaching business could pin an image showing two people in consultation and put a price that indicates an hour of time.

MARKETING MIX-UP

Put only one price on the pin. We once saw a pin with both a price and a shipping fee that was lower. The price showing on the corner of the pin was the lower-priced shipping fee, which was misleading to customers.

Naming Someone in Your Pins

Add the @ (at) symbol before a Pinterest username, such as @ babsinrome, to tag other Pinterest users in your description. This innovative networking opportunity lets you contact colleagues and build collaborative followings. It's a way of saying "Thought you'd like this," much like you might clip and pass on an article or send a website link via email.

Using Hashtags in Your Pins

When you write a description, use keywords as tags as you would on your blog, website, and tweets. These tags, or hashtags, make keywords in your descriptions searchable and are copied when a pin is repinned. Here's an example description using a hashtag:

> Johnson's #popcorn $10 for a 5 gallon tin. Just in time for #Christmas.

Use words or phrases other pinners are likely to use when searching for your type of company, product, or service so they can find your pins on Pinterest. You also want to use search terms that show up in general web search engines like Google and Yahoo! Google Analytics (google.com/analytics) can help you identify appropriate, unbranded keywords.

If you want a fun way to analyze your website copy to determine which words you use most, try the so-called toy Wordle (wordle.net). Essentially, you apply Wordle to text you've written, and Wordle creates a graphic of your most frequently used words. Those are the words you should be using as tags in your pin descriptions so both your pins and your website show up in web searches. Create catchy phrases using those specific, searchable words, and use names instead of euphemisms—for example, write "Dallas Cowboys" instead of "Texas' Finest."

MARKETING MIX-UP

Remember to deselect the **Hide your Pinterest profile from search engines** option in **Settings**. You *want* your tags to appear in search results.

Timing Your Pins

You might not think *when* you pin makes much of a difference, but it does.

Think of your pinning schedule the way you would your blogging schedule. With both, you need to be consistent so your followers know more or less when to expect to find new pins from you. Pinning regularly helps you enhance your brand and keep your followers engaged, while pinning too frequently might cause you to lose followers. Too-frequent contact is the number-one reason people unsubscribe from email newsletters and Facebook and Twitter updates.

Time your pins to just shortly before the hours when your customers are on Pinterest. As on other social networks, people tend to check in during the first hours of the day—a little Pinterest with your morning cup of coffee. The after-dinner hour is also Pinterest primetime. We know pinners who spend up to an hour before bedtime pinning and repinning because they find it relaxing to look through all the lovely pins before going to sleep.

Other Forms of Engagement

Like any social network, the foundation of Pinterest is creating community and sharing through following and collaboration. If you follow a fellow pinner, he is more likely to follow you. By engaging with pins from other pinners, you enhance your overall Pinterest presence and in turn build your brand recognition.

A clever way of mixing up your boards is to pin things from your clients' websites and blogs. If you have a business-to-business offering, you can court that client with Pinterest or develop a "Business We Want" board where you pin products from companies you want to work with. This helps define your brand image by letting people know what kind of clients you want to work with.

The most obvious form of engagement is repinning. If you repin a business, tagging the pinner or company in the description of the repin is a nice way of letting the business know you're spreading its message. But there are probably many beautiful pins that don't quite fit the objectives of your boards. Liking those pins is a terrific way to interact with those pins and pinners. Your likes are grouped together under the Likes tab on your Pinterest profile, and you or someone who visits your profile can view your likes—it's a way to get to know you.

VERY PINTERESTING!

A study conducted by RJ Metrics found that 80 percent of all pins are repins!

Leaving comments on pins affects not only your presence but also gives you another chance to develop your Pinterest identity. In keeping with Pinterest etiquette, your comments should be nice and written in clean language. That doesn't mean it has to be a compliment; it could be a question, an observation, or even constructive criticism. But don't be nasty, and please NO CAPITAL LETTERS, which is construed as yelling. You can also use @*username* in your comment to tag another pinner in the comment.

Link Reclamation

You know you have great products, and you pin them as part of your marketing efforts, but you might not think of them as particularly pinnable, at least by other pinners. You might be surprised, however, that pinners pin just about everything, and your products may have been pinned without the appropriate backlink to your website or online catalog.

You can search for pins showing your products by searching not only for your company and product name but also the generic name of your product and common misspellings.

If you find pins that don't link to your page but should, send a friendly message to the pinner by commenting directly on the pin. Mention you appreciate that they pinned your image but would be even more appreciative of a proper credit and backlink. If they don't respond, usually you can find a link to their Facebook or Twitter accounts by clicking the related icon on their Pinterest profile. Explain how to correct the link to the pinner (click the **Edit** button on the pin and change the URL), and thank them for taking the time to do this.

Unfortunately, changing the link on the original pin doesn't change the link on repins, so you'll have to contact anyone who repinned the image and ask them to edit the URL on the repin. If you run into problems, you can contact Pinterest and ask it to intervene. Be sure to provide both the erroneous URL and the correct one, as well as information about the pinner and board where the pin is found.

The Least You Need to Know

- Pin a balanced mix of images that show your products or services and images from other sources that convey the emotion or lifestyle your brand represents.

- Use images that are relevant to your brand and message, and remember to favor quality over quantity.

- Write descriptive pin descriptions to communicate and reinforce the key message you want followers to remember about your brand or product.

- Use price tags, @ (at) mentions, and # (hashtags) to make your pins more findable and to interact with followers.

- Time your pins to just before your customers are likely to log in so they appear toward the top of the opening Pinterest page.

- Engage with other pinners to increase your visibility by writing and responding to comments as well as liking and repinning a variety of pins.

- Reclaim misfiring links for your company and product images, and be sure to give credit where credit is due.

Implementing Your Pinterest Tactics

Now that you have a clear understanding of what this incredible visual social media platform is all about, it's time to start implementing what you've learned into concrete Pinterest tactics for your company.

Part 3 helps you actualize your newfound knowledge into a Pinterest plan you'll want to maintain on a daily basis. With all social media platforms, consistency is key, and Pinterest is no exception.

Because Pinterest does not exist in a vacuum, Chapter 9 goes over the importance of integrating Pinterest into the rest of your social media efforts, and teaches you how to make a pin soar across platforms. Chapter 10 provides critical pin knowledge of where to source great content, as well as useful tips on how to pin for a discriminating audience. Finally, Chapters 11 and 12 take you through the process of interacting and engaging with your Pinterest community in a fun and productive way.

Pinterest and Your Online Presence

In This Chapter

- Using Facebook to drive Pinterest traffic
- Using Twitter to drive Pinterest traffic
- Adding Pin It and Follow Me buttons
- Linking Pinterest around the web

The saying goes something like "any publicity is good publicity." We'd add "good publicity is *great* publicity." Any time someone sees, reads, or hears something about your company, brand, product, or service, the light of recognition in her brain gets a little brighter. And when customers are exposed to your company from a combination of media outlets, your bottom line improves. Adding Pinterest to your online marketing efforts helps increase your revenue.

According to a *Forbes* article (forbes.com/sites/ciocentral/2012/02/23/the-law-of-accelerating-media-and-how-to-deal-with-it), the Law of Accelerating Media explains the exponential acceleration of modes of media communication: 377 years passed from the time of print to radio, 71 years from radio to television, 42 years between the advent of television and the internet, and only 10 years have gone by between the internet and mobile and social media. Although the old technologies aren't replaced by the new technologies, their impact may be lessened. As we touched on in Chapter 5, the most effective marketing plan takes advantage of many media outlets. Pinterest is one of the most recent, with a presence in both web and mobile technologies.

In this chapter, we show you how to add the tools Pinterest provides to your website or blog. Then we explore some ideas for integrating various online media outlets to reinforce your brand and drive traffic to your site.

Linking Pinterest to Your Website and Blog

The first connection you want to make is to add a Pinterest link to your website and blog. You find tools to add link buttons on the Pinterest website in the **Goodies** section of the **Help** pages. You also want to have lots of great-quality images, including photos and infographics, on your website and blog so when things do get pinned from your website and blog, they represent you well.

> **VERY PINTERESTING!**
>
> Channels with higher visual and emotional resonance and social media cache are actually significant factors to drive higher revenue per order. … The presence of social media in a Purchase Path proved to drive higher value orders, in terms of revenue per order, than natural and paid search combined.
>
> —*A Guide to Market Leadership in 2012,* Clearsaleing, Columbus, Ohio

Adding the Pin It Button to Your Website

The **Pin It** button lets people who visit your website easily pin your images to their Pinterest boards. The function is similar to other social media buttons, such as those for Facebook or Twitter.

To add the **Pin It** button to your website, click **Pin It Button** from the **About** menu. Scroll down to the section **Pin It Button for Web Sites**. Type the requested information on the form:

- The URL of your web page
- The URL of the image that may be pinned

- A description of the pin (This is optional, but writing one tends to encourage more pinning because it makes pinning effortless.)

Click the **Pin Count** pull-down menu to choose where you want the number of times the image has been pinned appear:

- **Horizontal** displays the pin count number to the right of the button.
- **Vertical** displays the pin count number above the button.
- **No Count** displays the button alone.

*Copy the **Pin It** button to your website so viewers can pin to their Pinterest boards quickly and easily.*

The HTML code is automatically written to reflect the information you type in the form. Click and drag to select the code in the box, and copy and paste it next to the image on your website where you want the **Pin It** button to appear.

If you have multiple images on one page, such as a catalog or image-heavy article and you want to insert a **Pin It** button next to each image, complete the form for each image so the image URL is inserted in the code and then select, copy, and paste the code next to the relative image.

You also need to copy and paste the JavaScript to your web page— but only once—directly above the closing </BODY> tag, as instructed.

> **MARKETING MIX-UP**
>
> The **Pin It** button for your website is not the same as the **Pin It** button (sometimes called a bookmarklet or pinmarklet) you installed on your browser's bookmarks or favorites bar that facilitates pinning from sites to your boards. This button lets people pin images from your website to their Pinterest boards. It's the same idea, but geared toward others rather than you.

Adding the Follow Me Button to Your Blog or Website

The **Follow Me** button is a good way to let your blog readers know you're on Pinterest and introduce this social medium to those who don't know Pinterest.

In the **"Follow Button" for Websites** section, Pinterest offers four button styles for you to use. Click on the one you want to place on your website or blog, and the associated HTML code appears in a field to the right of the button. Click and drag over the code, and copy and paste it to your site. You can insert the buttons in your website or blog's text or in a sidebar.

> **VERY PINTERESTING!**
>
> You can see who has pinned items from your website by going to pinterest.com/source/*yourwebsiteURL*.

*The **Follow Me** button lets your readers know about your Pinterest presence.*

Adding the Pinterest Logo to Your Marketing Materials

Pinterest also shares its Pinterest logo for you to use. In the **Artwork** section, you can choose between the Pinterest logo and the Pinterest badge. You can download either EPS or PNG files for either graphic, and insert it in your digital and print marketing materials.

Much like the "Follow us on Twitter" and "Find us on Facebook" invitations, you can add a phrase such as "See our products on Pinterest" or "See what we're up to on Pinterest" to your website, and insert the logo.

If you don't have room for the entire logo or phrases, insert the badge next to the Facebook, Twitter, and any other badges you use.

Increasing a Pin's Visibility

In Chapter 8, we talked about using keywords in your pin descriptions so your pins show up in web searches. (That's the idea behind search engine optimization, or SEO.) You can also increase your pin's visibility by using other online media outlets to promote your Pinterest activity, and vice versa.

We mentioned the importance of a cohesive presence across all media outlets that are appropriate (and affordable) for your business. We also warned against nagging. You want to find the balance between subtly reminding your present and future customers about your brand without being obnoxiously in their face. You can accomplish this by having your brand show up intermittently in different places at different times and in different forms.

Each appearance is a chance to continue the conversation with your customer and grow your relationship. Think of traditional advertising such as print, television, and radio as ringing your customer's doorbell and introducing yourself. Your website or storefront says, "Nice to see you again. Here's what we do." Your blog says, "Sit down and stay a while," while Facebook, Twitter, and Pinterest are the perfect response when your customer says, "I only have a minute, so show me what's new," and with a few words or images, you show what you're up to.

On Your Blog

Pinterest and your blog are great promotional partners. In its simplest, passive form, you want to have the **Follow Me** button on your blog and the URL for your blog or website on your Pinterest profile.

Interesting things can happen when you use each to generate traffic on the other. When you post to your blog, include an image, and pin that image on a board. You could create a blog board where you pin all your blogs. If you write a blog that correlates to a themed board, pin it there, too. Nothing stops you from pinning the same thing on two different boards, especially if those two boards have different followings.

Use your blog as a Pinterest teaser. Put just one or two images on your blog, along with a descriptive post that points readers to your Pinterest board where they can see more related images. Be sure to include a permalink to your Pinterest board, and use permalinks on your pins to link back to the specific blog post.

Take a stroll around Pinterest to find inspiration for your blog, too. Look for trends within your niche but also in other areas that interest you. By blogging about corollary subjects, you can reach customers and influencers outside your normal circle. For example, you may sell shoes but you notice an architectural trend about sustainable energy. You could write a blog that links sustainability to shoes and post an *@username* comment on the pin that inspired your blog with a link to your blog. This lets followers of that board know they might find something interesting on your website, blog, and eventually your Pinterest boards.

Use the **Like** button to stockpile pins that inspire future blogs. You can even do a random exercise to like pins that hit you on an emotional or aesthetic level. Then take a look at the collection of likes you created to see if any trend or idea comes out of them.

We introduced you to Covington Aircraft in Chapter 5. We think it's combining blogging and Pinterest in a great way. Each pin on its "Aviation" board links to a blog or vlog post. Pinterest lets customers see an overview of all the blogs together, and the visual gives an immediate indication of the blog's focus.

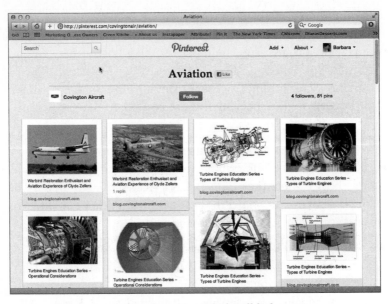

*Pin an image from your blog, which will link to your
blog when someone clicks on the enlarged pin image.*
(Covington Aircraft)

You might not associate the U.S. Army with marketing, but it does
indeed have a service that it's *selling*. The Army looks for recruits
and strives to maintain a good public image in the United States
and abroad. The Army's Pinterest profile tells you right in the
description that you'll find the "most recent news stories, videos,
and photos." Some of the pins are standalone, while others link to
websites and blogs. This profile is a great example of building boards
to meet different audience interests: you find boards as different as
"Basic Combat Training," "Army Style & Fashion," "Humanitarian
Relief," and "Going Green." We think this profile is worth studying.

MARKETING MIX-UP

Be sure your links are accurate when you set them up on Pinterest, your
website, or your blog. Don't just trust that you've typed in the correct
URL—test it, too. You don't want misfiring links!

Pinterest can serve as a hub for linking to other places on the web where you have a presence.
(U.S. Army)

On Facebook

You want to activate the automatic Facebook update on Pinterest, if you didn't during the initial setup. (Go to **Edit Profile** on your profile page and check the **Link to Facebook** box.) Use your Facebook status updates to nudge your Facebook friends to check out major Pinterest changes.

Olive Farm is the Facebook identity for author, actress, and film-maker Carol Drinkwater. Ms. Drinkwater has built a large, friendly Facebook community and has recently established a Pinterest presence, and her frequent Facebook postings prompt friends to look at her pins on Pinterest. Her Pinterest profile description mentions what she does and cites both the URL for her website as well as the email to contact her about buying her books, DVDs, or photos. Her pins show images of the lifestyle and issues portrayed in her books and films, creating a compelling and cohesive message.

Use Facebook postings to lead people to your Pinterest page, which offers an easier way to view photos.

(© Carol Drinkwater, caroldrinkwater.com)

Use the profile description to let people know what you do and how to reach you.

(photos: © Carol Drinkwater, 2012; jacket cover images for books for younger readers: © Orion Publishing Group UK; jacket cover images for Olive Farm books: © Scholastic UK)

On Twitter

When you set up your Pinterest profile, you probably activated the automatic Twitter link so a tweet is sent when you update your pins. If you didn't choose this option, do it now. (Go to your profile page. Click **Edit Profile**, and check the **Link to Twitter** box to link your Pinterest and Twitter accounts.)

Tweet to announce special updates like new boards that reflect seasonal happenings or new additions to your company employee roster. You can also include the image from one of the pins on the board in your tweet to appeal to the immediate, visceral reaction your followers will have to images.

When you tweet about other business events, mention that you can see visual details on Pinterest because, of course, you'll be building a board about that business event, too.

> **PIN TIP**
>
> Consider it a goodwill effort to use both Facebook and Twitter to mention pins from other sources. It's like saying, "Look what I found. I think you'll find it (P)interesting, too." Remember to include *@username* in the tweet to let the source know you're promoting them.

On LinkedIn

LinkedIn is the professional's social network. Although on the surface it might look like it provides traditional links between companies and people looking for jobs, it's also a great source to introduce yourself to potential clients if you're a freelancer or contractor who offers a service.

What does this have to do with Pinterest? Think about the difference between a black-and-white résumé or bio and a colorful presentation of projects you've worked on or a video presentation of you. You can create boards that showcase your experience and put a Pinterest link on your LinkedIn profile.

If you're a project manager, pin images of the stages of the project or create a graphic of the process. Of course, whatever you create for Pinterest can and should be used on your website or posted on Facebook, too.

Tyler Cheese is a young copywriter who pinned his résumé in a very unique way (pinterest.com/teecheese). He used the first four boards to make a banner across his profile, and each board in the second row contains pins that highlight the parts of his résumé. Each pin on the Social Media board is a link to his profile on different online communities, such as Facebook, Twitter, and LinkedIn.

> **PIN TIP**
>
> Take photos and make videos of works in progress, and use them as part of your marketing story. The popularity of reality shows attests to the fact that people literally want to know your business, who you are, and how you do it.

On Twitpic, Instagram, and Flickr

Pinterest is such a visual site, it's a natural fit to pin from images you post on Twitpic (twitpic.com), Instagram (instagr.am), Flickr (flickr. com), or other social photo-sharing networks. Some, like Instagram, give you the opportunity to easily enhance your images and instantly share across the other social media outlets you use.

The advantage here is uploading to one site and then sharing rather than uploading multiple times. If you have a lot of images, you can pin some of them and encourage followers to go to the original site to view lengthier slideshows.

Does This Apply to Your Business?

If you're shaking your head and thinking, *This is great, but it doesn't apply to my business,* think again. Throughout this book, we use examples from different business sectors, and in the following sections, we show two more companies from different business sectors that are using an integrated approach. Browse Pinterest, and you'll find many more sectors represented, from international companies in education, publishing, business services, and consumer products to local service providers such as hair salons, spas, hardware stores, and real estate agents.

ZAGGDaily

ZAGGDaily is the Pinterest account for tech product company ZAGG, which builds Pinterest boards around its tweets. People who follow ZAGG's tweets can view them on Pinterest, and Pinterest followers can subscribe to ZAGG's Twitter feed.

Let people know your business is on different social media platforms by cross-referencing them.
(ZAGG, Inc.)

The board description invites viewers to tweet the ZAGG social media manager with questions. This is a terrific way to start and keep the conversation open.

ZAGG's profile also showcases other tech gadgets it thinks are cool, which puts it in our "Good Pinterest Practice" category. ZAGG has two other profiles: iFrogz, which concentrates on its iPhone and iPad product line, and ZAGG International, the parent company.

Southwest Airlines

Southwest Airlines is building a following by communicating how it does what it does in images pinned from a variety of original Southwest sources, such as its blog, Instagram, and Webstagram (web.stagram.com). The following figure shows its "Vintage" board, but it installs a sense of customer service and added value in other boards that offer packing and travelling tips as well as ideas for making things in the shape of an airplane.

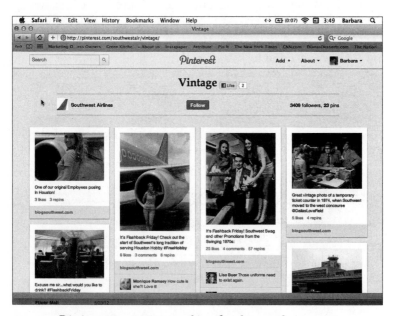

Dig in to your company archives for photos and graphics from the past that show the longevity and evolution of your business.
(Southwest Airlines)

Schoolhouse Review Crew

The Schoolhouse Review Crew boards, curated by *The Old School-house* magazine, offers information about homeschooling and pins reviews of homeschooling products. Pins on *The Old Schoolhouse* magazine board link to the magazine itself as well as blogs and other services for homeschoolers. This is just one example of education exchanges that happen on Pinterest.

If your business has multiple offerings—even on the same website—make a pin to link to each offering, and add links to complementary sites, too
(© 2012 *The Old Schoolhouse*® Magazine, LLC, PO Box 8426, Gray, TN 37615)

The Least You Need to Know

- Be sure your pins are cited on Facebook and Twitter, and consider other social media opportunities, such as LinkedIn, where you can reach your customers.
- Add the **Pin It** and **Follow Me** buttons to your website and blog, and encourage visitors to your site to look at your Pinterest profile.

- Write blogs that push readers to Pinterest and vice versa, and remember the opportunity to post video from YouTube or Vimeo to Pinterest.

- Create a cohesive, compelling identity and message that's reinforced by your words and images across all social media, print, and electronic communications.

Sourcing Stellar Pins

Chapter 10

In This Chapter

- Establishing your pin sources
- Pinning from multiple sources
- The places where great pins lie
- Becoming a discerning pinner
- Educational and informative pins

One thing that should be explicitly clear by now is the fact that pinning beautiful images on Pinterest is pretty much the name of the game. And while this might seem like a simple task for the visually inclined, it's not as easy as it seems. You might be nodding your head in agreement at this very moment.

One of the most common questions pinners and soon-to-be pinners ask Christine is "Where do you find all of those gorgeous images you pin?" This question is generally followed by the statement, "You must spend hours and hours searching all over the web!" Christine is a bit of a web addict, so this statement is true. She does spend a considerable amount of time combing the web for great content. But she also has go-to sources she visits when she wants to do some quick pinning.

In this chapter, we go over some great resources to pull pins from as well as some great tips on how to keep pinning in dynamic and interesting ways.

Why Create Pin Sources?

If you've spent some time browsing Pinterest, you've probably realized you can easily lose several hours of your day being mesmerized by pretty pictures. We've been there. In fact, it happens frequently. And once you start contributing to Pinterest by pinning your favorite (and brand-relevant) content, you'll find that you can lose hours of time actively pinning, too.

Pinterest is a great place to escape for a little while, but losing hours at a time could prove to be detrimental. And what successful businessperson can afford that?

That's why we've created bookmarked *pin sources* for ourselves. This is a collection of our favorite ecommerce sites, blogs, and photo-resource sites we frequently visit and pin from. As we've mentioned throughout this book, contributing to Pinterest every day is important when establishing, building, and maintaining your brand presence on this site. But time is a precious commodity. So to stay on top of your pinning duties while ensuring you have plenty of time to take care of other tasks, you're going to find that having bookmarked pin sources is extremely helpful.

DEFINITION

Pin sources are an organized collection of bookmarked websites where you can find guaranteed content to pin with ease.

Keeping your pin sources organized is the key. We like to organize our bookmarked resources by subject categories that complement the variety of boards we have on Pinterest. For example, we have a bookmarked folder full of links to our favorite food sites, fashion blogs, ecommerce sites, etc. because those are some of the main topics we like to cover on Pinterest.

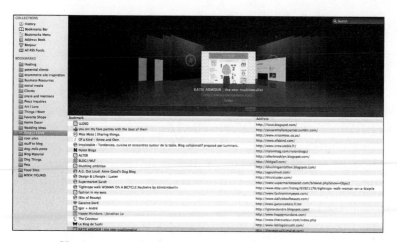

Here's an example of Christine's bookmarked folders
where she stores her pin sources according to category.

A lot of Pinterest users like to use their own pins as pin sources. So when they're searching for content to pin, they follow the links on some of their favorite pins back to the original websites. This can work as well, but we find that archiving favorite websites in organized folders is a much more efficient way of keeping pin sources organized.

In addition, by breaking down your pin sources by topic—food, fashion, interior spaces, travel, etc.—you're more conscious of keeping your pin stream dynamic and mixing up the content of your pins. (If you're wondering what a pin stream is, don't worry. We cover that later in this chapter.)

Keeping Source Variety in Mind

Something you want to avoid when you're pinning on Pinterest is pinning from the same source too often. Whether that source is your own website or blog, or someone else's site you admire, pinning from one source too frequently won't help you look like a knowledgeable pinner. On Pinterest, you have the ability to curate all the wonderful things you find on the internet, not all of the wonderful things you find on one website. It's critical to keep source variety in mind when you're pinning.

MARKETING MIX-UP

Pinning from a single source on the internet too frequently is not a good pinning practice. Pin content from a variety of sources so you appear more well informed to your fellow pinners.

Pin sources can also include the pin content you repin from pinners you follow. As we discuss later in this chapter, other pinners can be amazing sources of content, which is why following great pinners with shared interests is important. But be sure you aren't constantly repinning from just one or two of your favorite pinners. Much like with being careful not to pin all your original Pinterest content from one website, be careful not to repin all your content from one or two users. Keeping source variety in mind when repinning is just as important!

Creating a Dynamic Pin Stream

Now let's talk about your *pin stream*. A pin stream is the pin view you get when you look at your profile through your pins (pinterest. com/*yourwebsiteURL*/pins). This particular profile view enables you to view your pins in the order in which you've pinned them, in a continuous stream, with the most recent pins at the top.

DEFINITION

Your **pin stream** is the continuous stream of pins you can see when you view a profile through **Pins** (pinterest.com/*yourwebsiteURL*/pins). In a pin stream view, pins appear with the most recent up top.

You can also view other users' pin streams by visiting their profile and clicking on **Pins** on the drop-down list under their avatar. We enjoy viewing a pinner's Pinterest account this way, and we're not alone! Several pinners we've spoken with have found this is a great way to quickly get a sense of the content a particular pinner is curating. Visiting each and every board on a profile can take quite a bit of time, depending on how many boards an individual or a company has. When pinners are making decisions about whom they want to follow, many times they'll scroll through that pinner's most recent pins. If the content is consistently strong, typically they'll elect to follow all.

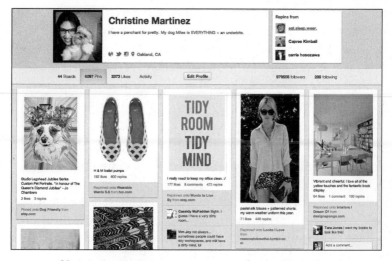

Christine's pin stream covers a range of topics like illustrations, inspirational word art, and fashion.

Because so many users look to a pinner's pin stream when they're making the decision to follow or not, maintaining variation throughout your pin stream is a great idea. Variation in this case doesn't necessarily mean a variation in pin sources; rather, we mean variation on content.

PIN TIP

Keeping your pin stream dynamic with several different types of pins shows your range of pin content to other pinners.

We've established that pins in a pin stream appear in the order in which they were pinned. No matter what board they're categorized under, in a pin stream, all pins appear together.

Keeping this in mind, let's say you have a board that consists of your favorite furniture pieces. If you were to pin 10 pieces of furniture in a row, those pins would appear in your pin stream all together. If a potential follower were to come along and view your pin stream, he would immediately see that you like to pin a lot of furniture.

But what if you actually pin a lot of food recipes, too, and you primarily focus on food industry content? Potential followers who come across your pin stream full of furniture might not know that about you. They could investigate further by taking a look at your boards, but most people move along quickly on the internet, and they might just pass you by based on the most recent content you've put forth, not on the content you've collected over time.

To avoid losing potential followers by having too many similar content pins in a row, keep your pin stream dynamic. Mix up the content you pin every time you sit down for a Pinterest session. If you've got 15 different boards, be sure you throw a pin to each board. That keeps your pin stream from looking stale and driven by one particular interest. A great pin stream looks very diverse, yet somehow it all works together because it represents one person's taste (yours) or one brand's aesthetic (your company).

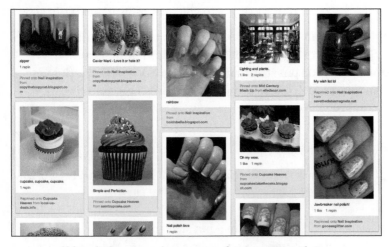

Although this pinner has a range of unique topics, their pin stream shows a limited view of cupcakes and nail polish designs.

Where to Find Great Pin Content

The internet is a massive place, and you can find amazing pin content on it just about anywhere. However, some very specific websites and places online offer great pin content. In this section, we share some photo-driven websites you're going to want to head over to time and time again when you sit down to pin.

PIN TIP

With the exception of blogs, some of the websites discussed in the following sections require you to create an account to use the site. But don't worry, it's free and easy to sign up.

Blogs

Blogs are one of our favorite places to find great content to pin. Blog writers and editors curate the best of the internet within the topic they blog about. Depending on the content and quality of a blog, you can usually count on your favorite bloggers to post and write about material that's pinworthy.

In addition, establishing a relationship with the blogger can potentially lead to them blogging about a reader's services, products, or expertise. Pinterest is also about community, so building relationships is an important marketing benefit, too.

There are millions of blogs online, covering just about any topic you can think of, so when you're searching for blogs to pin from that cover your particular interests, look for blogs that are photo driven.

Victoria Smith of sfgirlbybay writes and curates for an image-driven blog full of pinnable imagery.

Tumblr

Tumblr (tumblr.com) is a blogging platform that mostly consists of short, image-driven posts. Because Tumblr is a short form of blogging, much of the text you'd otherwise see on a blog post is cut out, and communication is done through the photos posted—kind of like Pinterest. Given the nature of this particular blogging platform, great pinworthy images are easy to find.

Tumblr blogs are searchable by topic, so find your favorite Tumblr blogs that correspond with your interests and Pinterest topics, and pin away!

Tumblr blogs, like this one, focus on image-driven posts as opposed to traditional word-driven blogs.

StumbleUpon

StumbleUpon (stumbleupon.com) is an easy-to-use website that helps you discover new and interesting stuff on the web focused around your interests. Based on what you "like," StumbleUpon points you in the direction of great web pages that you might not have found on your own.

For those of you who need a little assistance navigating the web, StumbleUpon can be a great service, leading you to websites you'll want to bookmark as your go-to pin sources.

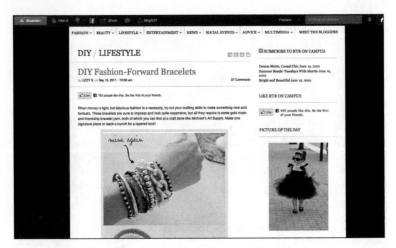

*Based on Christine's interests, StumbleUpon found
a great fashion blog, from Rent The Runway, full of
pinnable content she loves.*

Delicious

Delicious (delicious.com) is a place to collect and showcase your
passions from across the web. This site enables you to save what you
like on topics of interest and compile them into one themed "stack"
for easy sharing.

To find pinworthy content, you can browse through the stacks
belonging to other users who have similar interests to your own.
When you find links to cool websites, you're likely to find content
you can't wait to pin.

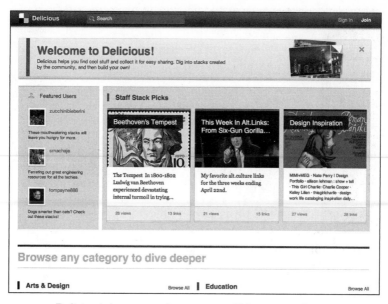

Delicious's home page shows some staff favorite stacks that will help you get started with your search.

FFFFOUND!

FFFFOUND! (ffffound.com) is a web service that allows users to post and share their favorite images "found" on the web, and recommends those images to other users with similar tastes and interests. The more you define your tastes, the better your personal recommendations become.

This site also allows you to bookmark the images you like. With topic-geared, high-quality images being recommended to you daily, FFFFOUND! is a great source for pinworthy content, and will probably end up directing you to websites you'll pin from again and again.

FFFFOUND! continuously feeds its users great, high-quality images ideal for Pinterest.

We Heart It

We Heart It (weheartit.com) is an easy-to-navigate site full of images its users have found, tagged, and organized on the site. Millions of great images can be found here, and they're simple to find through search terms. For example, if you type in "dogs," you'll get hundreds of pages full of adorable doggie images. We Heart It is one of our favorite photo-sharing websites to visit for "pinspiration."

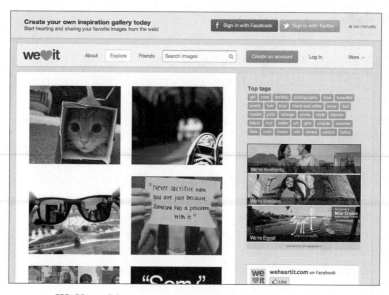

*We Heart It's images are all tagged and easy to search.
Type in a subject on the search tab, and enjoy the
thousands of images generated.*

Facebook, Twitter, and Google+

Social networking sites like Facebook, Twitter, and Google+ are also
great sites to find content for pins. It's not uncommon for someone
within your network to post great content you love and want to
share. And on occasion, they may even post something or direct you
to a website with pinnable content.

Keeping your eyes peeled and allowing your friends and contacts to
guide you to cool places on the web is a great idea—and it takes the
job off you for a little while. Christine, for example, often pins great
products some of her favorite fashion bloggers post on Twitter.

Pinterest

Last but certainly not least, Pinterest is now the best place to find pinnable content. In fact, as of March 2012, 80 percent of all pins on Pinterest are actually repins. That means the vast majority of Pinterest users are using Pinterest itself as a place to find great content. It might seem like a simple solution to only look to Pinterest when searching for pinnable images, but there's a lot of value in adding original content to the site.

If you're going to rely on repinning for a lot of your own Pinterest content, be prepared to apply the same rules of curation when you search for repinworthy content. Not all the content pinned on Pinterest is suitable for repinning. In fact, a lot of it isn't. As mentioned earlier, that's one of the primary reasons why you want to follow other pinners who not only share your interests, but who also put forth high-quality, repinnable images.

Pinning with an "Editor's Eye"

Most people probably underestimate how much thought goes into a beautiful Pinterest account. Pinners who are truly discerning about the content they put forth often spend a fair amount of time deciding whether or not a potential pin will not only maintain but enhance the high quality of pins that already exist on their boards.

To these selective and tasteful pinners, their Pinterest accounts are something like an exquisite and well-edited magazine, where readers can get excited for the lovely images and products they know were carefully sourced and selected. If your goal is to create an alluring Pinterest account—and it should be—you're going to want to be sure you're pinning with an editor's eye.

What does it mean to pin with an "editor's eye"? Think about what the editor of your favorite magazine does. One of her roles is to carefully select the best of what's presented and choose the right content for a particular issue of a magazine. Her colleagues and audience rely on her level of taste and judgment, and know with her in charge, they'll have a great product, issue after issue. It's important that she carefully considers the material she selects and put her best foot forward every time.

Dree Harper, Refinery29 contributor and creator of the fashion blog Create That Style, demonstrates exactly what it is to pin with an editorial eye. Each and every one of her pins bursts with high style. No matter what topic Dree covers, she chooses high-impact and vibrant photos that are the epitome of eye candy. Because she has such a distinct point of view, Dree's pinboards look more like a stylish magazine any woman would want to spend hours flipping through. Dree Harper's Pinterest account is proof positive that pinning with an editorial eye makes for a standout Pinterest presence.

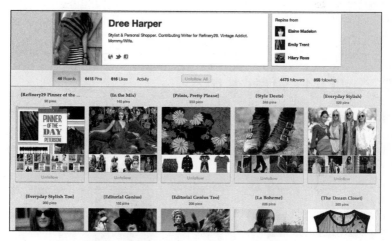

Dree Harper's Pinterest boards are full of stunning editorial-like content that resembles a well-edited magazine.

Saving "Likes" as Potential Pins

Pinning with an editorial eye means it's important to refrain from pinning anything and everything that catches your eye. And naturally, that goes for repins as well.

When combing through Pinterest to look for repinnable content, we like to use just as much thought as we do when we're scanning the web for images to pin. Occasionally, we come across an image or a product we're excited to pin immediately. But other times, we find that we're a bit unsure if the pin is worth pinning.

Off Pinterest, you can always leave several windows open and come back to potential pins later. But what do you do when you're scanning through Pinterest and something catches your eye that you're a bit unsure of? How do you come back to pins you might want to pin at another time?

You can use Pinterest's "like" function to keep pins you like, but you're not sure you want to repin, in your like stream. Similar to your pin stream, your like stream is the view of pins you've liked. You can view this stream when you click on **Likes** on your profile bar.

Using the like function is a great way to hold on to a pin you might want to pin at another time. Remember, repinning everything that catches your eye isn't a great Pinterest practice, but there's nothing wrong with liking everything you, well, like!

MARKETING MIX-UP

Everything you like on Pinterest is visible to all users on Pinterest, should they elect to view your like stream. Because of this, you should use caution when liking material on Pinterest that may be offensive to your customers and clients.

Sourcing Useful and Informative Pins

Some of the most popular pins on Pinterest go beyond just being a pretty image. They provide Pinterest followers with useful information by linking to tutorials, news stories, DIY instructions, and recipes. These types of informative pins go above and beyond the normal Pinterest pin, and it's no wonder they're among the most frequently shared and repinned. Because of their popularity, informative pins can add a lot of value to your brand's Pinterest presence.

These types of pins are slightly different from your stunning image or product pins, so it's important to know how and where to find these types of pins.

YouTube and Vimeo

With great video tutorials abundantly available on just about any and every topic you could imagine, YouTube and Vimeo are two sites full of useful and informative pins. You can mix videos in with any of your boards, but we recommend creating a specific board or boards for video content. That way, your followers know exactly where to find your interesting and informative video pins.

Don't forget to keep your video pins brand relevant, and be sure you keep this content creative. For example, if your company sells fitness accessories, pin workout videos or tutorials revolving around great health practices. If your company sells boats, pin videos about safe boating practices, how-to fishing tips for beginners, or knot-tying for sailors.

General Electric likes to incorporate informative video pins in creative ways throughout its various Pinterest boards. From "Archives," where it posts past General Electric commercials, to "Badass Machines," where it entertains its followers with cool and fascinating videos on brilliant technological advances in machinery, GE has a great understanding of how to use useful and informative pins to enhance its brand presence on Pinterest.

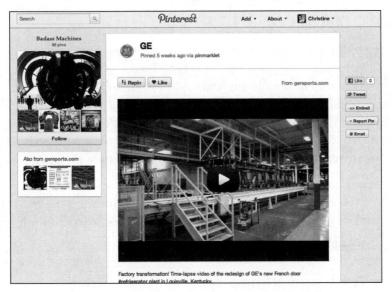

This cool and compelling video pin is on-brand for GE.

Blogs

Blogs based around niche topics are another excellent source for useful and informative pins. Many bloggers enjoy sharing DIY projects, software tutorials like tips and tricks on using Photoshop, favorite downloadable projects, and food recipes. If a blog is particularly attractive and well executed, the image pin leading to the tutorial will most likely be visually striking as well. Finding niche blogs that are attractive is key here.

Recipes and DIY projects are extremely popular on Pinterest, which makes sense, given the current site demographics. But food and recipe pins that are particularly attractive fare better than unattractive recipe pins.

Spoon Fork Bacon, for example, is an absolutely stunning food blog that shares a variety of different recipes. Not only are the food recipes unique, the food photography looks like something you'd see in an expensive cookbook.

This beautiful food photography pin (with recipe) is likely to be pinned and repinned repeatedly.

The combination of a beautiful pin and a linked tutorial makes for a perfect repinnable storm, and the chances of this pin's reach going far is highly probable. When you pin useful and informative pins from a blog, be sure the beautiful visual factor exists.

Web Publications

Web publications are often full of useful and informative pin possibilities. Like print publications, most web publications incorporate a fair amount of lifestyle content complementary to the topic at hand. For example, housing web publications often have home décor tips, storage ideas, how-to's, and DIY projects that can be done at home for the home owner on a budget. With millions of web publications in existence, it's not hard to find a few that would be relevant to your industry. Spending some time sorting through the best ones out there will prove to be valuable once you start pinning the informative material you find.

Most print publications now have a corresponding web publication with additional information and articles you won't find in the magazine. *Glamour* magazine online has a particularly strong division, Glamour Beauty, that provides weekly articles and how-to tips for hair, makeup, and everything else beauty related. The article images are also quite lovely, making this the perfect place to get useful and informative pinformation.

This hair how-to tutorial from Glamour *magazine's online publication is prime for pinning.*

The Least You Need to Know

- Having an archive of websites you like to pin from is a good way to make pinning sessions efficient.

- Rather than pin from a limited number of web sources, pin from a variety of sources to appear as a well-informed pinner.

- Creating a dynamic pin stream with mixed content gives potential followers a good sense of what you generally pin.

- Image-focused websites such as Tumblr, FFFFOUND!, and StumbleUpon are great places to source strong visual content for Pinterest, as are social platforms like Facebook and Twitter.

- Refrain from pinning anything and everything that catches your eye; focus on pinning in a discerning manner.

- Pins that link to useful information—such as how-to's, recipes, DIY projects, and even videos—are very popular and highly repinnable on Pinterest.

Strategic Following

In This Chapter

- Making smart "follow" decisions
- Developing a Pinterest presence
- Being a great Pinterest citizen
- Pinterest follow do's and don'ts

When you're in the process of building a strong presence within social media platforms, you'll inevitably find that there's a lot more strategy involved than you probably first imagined. Unless you're a big brand with an established fan base, building a large following for your company on a platform like Pinterest can be both challenging and time-consuming. In fact, in our experience so far, building a following on Pinterest generally takes more time and effort to achieve than it does on social media platforms like Facebook and Twitter.

Even with its challenges, building a large following on Pinterest isn't impossible. In this chapter, we provide some strategic tips on how to start to build your following and whom your brand should be following. We also go over some important Pinterest etiquette you're going to want to abide by. After all, a polite pinner is one who earns a following.

Choosing Whom to Follow

Being choosy about whom to follow on Pinterest is important. Strategy is key when you're building a brand presence on Pinterest, and whom you follow is a major part of that strategy.

The Importance of Being Selective

First and foremost, brands should always be selective when choosing whom to follow. That goes for Pinterest and on any other social platform. A brand's following list typically speaks volumes for that company. For example, if your company indiscriminately follows anyone, seasoned social media users might view this as an attempt to rack up followers. And that, to most, is a social media turn-off.

A brand should have a bit of an exclusivity factor when populating its follow list. By nature, we all want to get into that cool club or high-profile restaurant few can get in to. Creating that type of exclusivity for your brand's follow list will generally have others clamoring to get in. And how do users grab the attention of a brand they love? They talk about that brand! It's a great idea to keep those who love your company chatting you up across social media platforms.

When choosing whom to follow, start with your company's existing contacts and the people your brand follows on your other social media platforms. Chances are you follow them for a good reason, and whether you meant to be or not, you were selective when choosing these contacts, so some exclusivity already exists.

Fortunately, Pinterest has made it simple to follow and invite existing contacts from other social media platforms. You can search for and invite your contact from Facebook under your profile settings.

Alternatively, you can also search for and invite your contact list from Gmail and Yahoo! This is a great way of searching for the clients and customers you have on your mailing list.

*Pinterest automatically pulls up a list of your Facebook
friends who are using Pinterest.*

*Just like with your Facebook contacts, Pinterest enables
you to find both your Gmail and Yahoo! contacts who are
using the site.*

A brand's follow list can also serve as a great guide to those who follow you. It's yet another place your company can let its curatorial skills shine on Pinterest. As of this writing, Pinterest isn't an easy place to search for brands and other users you might be interested in following. That's where a company's follow list can solidify you as a trusted resource.

For example, Christine relies on brands she loves to find out who she should be following. This is easy to do by looking at the list of users they follow. Because she admires and respects their taste, she often uses her favorite brands as a great resource on this front as well.

Lucky Magazine has been one of Christine's favorite fashion publications for several years. She knows she can always rely on it for the hottest trends, and it can be a great resource for fashion purchases she'd like to make. The editors of *Lucky Magazine* are true cultivators of style on Pinterest as well. Because she's always searching for stellar Pinterest users in the fashion industry to follow, Christine likes to check out *Lucky Magazine*'s Pinterest follow list to find those individuals and brands she may not have found on her own.

Lucky Magazine *is following a great list of stylish Pinterest users who are ideal for those looking for fashionable pinners.*

Not only has *Lucky Magazine* become a great resource of repinnable content for her, it's also an invaluable resource when she's looking for new pinners to follow. If it was a brand that indiscriminately followed anyone it came across, this experience would be lost. And yes, Christine is hoping that by mentioning *Lucky Magazine* in this book, she'll grab their attention and they'll follow her on Pinterest.

PIN TIP

Being selective about who to follow on Pinterest is a great practice and helps create an air of exclusivity for your brand. This will have users you choose to follow appreciate your following them even more! Those you haven't chosen to follow will be vying for your attention by talking up your brand across social media platforms.

Grabbing Attention by Following

Some Pinterest users have incredibly large numbers of followers, and brands love to grab these users' attention. A pin or a repin from one of these power pinners can potentially drive large amounts of traffic to your brand's website. It can also result in some great exposure for your company profile on Pinterest, and that's a great way to pick up several new followers. Choosing to follow a power pinner is a great idea, particularly if your company reflects the interests of that pinner.

As an early adopter, Christine has been fortunate enough to accumulate a very large following on Pinterest. And from personal experience, she can say that simply following a power pinner on Pinterest isn't enough to necessarily grab their attention, particularly when that power pinner has around a million other followers. If a brand was hoping to get Christine's attention by simply following her on Pinterest, there's a high probability she wouldn't even notice.

That's not to go against our previous statement that following a power pinner is a good idea—it is! You're just going to have to work a bit harder to get that pinner's attention.

To get the attention of a power pinner you're following, use the @ mention to say hello and direct the power pinner's attention over to your company. If your brand represents something of interest to that pinner, she will be glad you introduced yourself. If your company isn't relevant to that power pinner's interests, offer a cool pin instead. If you pin something that pinner would enjoy, let him know with a "Hi @powerpinner! This looks like something you'd like." A repin from a power pinner is great exposure for your company.

Within most Pinterest profiles, you'll find links directing you to other places on the web to find a particular user. If you really think a power pinner should take a look at your company, follow one or more of those links and contact him. A friendly email or tweet is never a bad thing. And if that power pinner responds enthusiastically, both you and the power pinner will be glad you took the time to reach out.

Leave a nice and thoughtful comment on a power pinner's pin. If something she pinned caught your eye and you have a great comment to leave, leave it. More power pinners actually take the time to read all their comments than you think. When a comment is thoughtful, useful, or interesting, power pinners pay attention.

Just be sure not to go overboard with your comments. Leaving too many comments across multiple pins can become annoying.

PIN TIP

Using the @ symbol is a great way to grab another pinner's attention and direct it to a pin you'd like to share with them.

Following to Edit Your View

When you log on to Pinterest, you see all the most recent pins from pinners you follow. Imagine you were to follow thousands of pinners on Pinterest, whose interests and pin content you didn't carefully review before you hit "follow." What would Pinterest look like to you every time you logged on? It would look like the Pinterest "everything" page.

The Pinterest "everything" page displays a random collection of images that have most recently been pinned.

Scrolling through everything, you'll most likely find a fantastic gem of a pin that catches your eye, is relevant to your interests, and may even be repinnable. But for the most part, the view you get is a hodgepodge of random pins spanning a variety of different topics. You'd have to spend a considerable amount of time scrolling down the page before you found something you like. Overall, your own Pinterest experience would be a lot less enjoyable. And if your experience of Pinterest is unenjoyable, chances are you won't want to invest a whole lot of time on this platform.

Pinterest is all about curating and editing. And that goes for the users you choose to follow as well. When you log on to Pinterest, you want to see a continuous stream of high-quality content on topics that interest you. Weeding out users who continually add content that dilutes your Pinterest stream is a good idea. Instead, choose to follow those pinners who enhance your overall experience by providing you with stimulating eye candy, directing you to websites you're happy to discover, and giving you repinnable content for your own Pinterest account.

Just in case you're not completely sold on being judicious when choosing whom to follow on Pinterest, we want to share an anecdote with you. Recently, Christine left her laptop on at work with her

Pinterest account open as a very visible window on her screen. A co-worker couldn't help but look over and check out her Pinterest stream of pins. When Christine came back to sit down, her co-worker said, "Wow! What you see on Pinterest is so much prettier than what I see! Who are you following?" In an instant, her co-worker realized the importance of following great pinners.

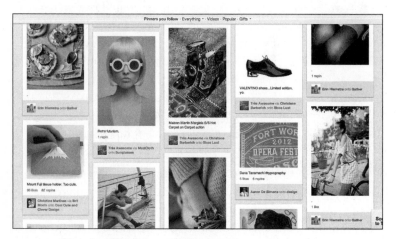

Christine follows several pinners with great taste who provide her with a beautiful view of Pinterest.

Building a Following

As we mentioned at the beginning of this chapter, building a large following on Pinterest is a challenging endeavor, and it can take a lot of time and effort to acquire. This can be especially true for small businesses and brands that aren't able to come into Pinterest with large followings from other social media platforms. We like to think of a following on Pinterest as being a truly earned following. You must put forth high-quality content every time you pin in order to catch the eye of other pinners. A strong following doesn't come easily; it's something you have to work hard to earn.

Challenging as it may be, there are definitely some things you can do to help your Pinterest following grow. First, tie in your existing social networks by letting your followers on other platforms know you're now on Pinterest. Does your company send out newsletters? If so, be sure to mention your company's new Pinterest account to get your mailing list excited about following you. Once you're on Pinterest, you can invite as many people as you'd like to join. Take advantage of this by offering Pinterest invitations to customers and clients on your mailing list.

Engage with other pinners with the @ mention and by leaving thoughtful comments. We mentioned this as a tactic to grab the attention of a power pinner, but this is also a great way of getting anyone on Pinterest to notice you. But remember, don't overwhelm pinners with too many comments. Christine once had a pinner leave a comment on every one of her pins on a particular board. She sure got Christine's attention, but not in a positive way. Also, when you do decide to leave a comment, be sure to keep it short and sweet. Longwinded comments will likely go unread and may be perceived as annoying.

Pin with regularity and on a schedule your followers will come to rely on. We can't stress this point enough. When you're in the process of building a following, it's important to be sure you're putting forth great pins every day. You'll find that your following grows much more quickly if you do.

Pin original content. As mentioned in Chapter 10, currently 80 percent of pins on Pinterest are repins. Become a Pinterest standout by pinning your own internet finds and bringing something new to the Pinterest table. Other pinners will start to notice your unique point of view and content contributions.

Make all aspects of your Pinterest account searchable. Whether it's your individual pins or the titles of your boards, be sure you're using keywords and tagging them with hashtags. One of the more popular ways Pinterest users find new accounts to follow is by searching the site with keywords and phrases. Integrating relevant keywords throughout your Pinterest content helps make you a more visible pinner.

Use the source pin URL (pinterest.com/source/*yourwebsiteURL*) to find Pinterest users who have pinned content from your website. Spend some time, on occasion, commenting on these pins with a simple "Thanks for pinning!" comment. Oftentimes, users will pin from your website without realizing you're on Pinterest. Showing that pinner that you appreciate their pinned support not only lets them know you're on Pinterest, it could potentially turn a fan into a follower.

MARKETING MIX-UP

Building a substantial following on Pinterest is challenging and time-consuming, particularly if you're a small company. Don't let a slow growth rate to your follow count discourage you from continuing to build your Pinterest presence. Hang in there, and keep pinning. Once you start to gain momentum and new followers, you'll be happy you stuck with it.

Abiding by Pinterest's Top Three Rules

For an overall positive Pinterest experience, good pin etiquette should be a top priority. It's especially important to maintain good pin etiquette and play by the Pinterest rules if you represent a company.

Just as you'd be careful not to post or tweet anything that would bring negative attention your way on Facebook or Twitter, keeping your brand from breaking the Pinterest rules ensures that you stay in good standing with the Pinterest community at large. As stated on the official Pinterest website "Pin Etiquette" page, "Pinterest is special because of the people that use it."

To be sure you're abiding by Pinterest's top three rules, it's important that you know and understand each rule. It's amazing to see how often one or more of these rules is broken by even the most well-intentioned pinner. Periodically review the rules and remind yourself to maintain good Pinterest etiquette at all times.

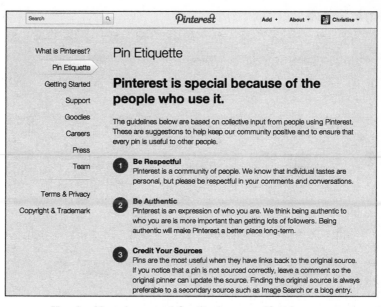

You should read over and familiarize yourself with Pinterest's top three rules.

Rule 1: Be Respectful

Pinterest is a community of people who openly showcase the things they love, find interesting, and that reflect their personal taste. Chances are, you'll come across pins that make you scratch your head a bit and seriously question that pinner's taste. You also may see something you vehemently disagree with.

But no matter how much you dislike that pinner's content, if she is not pinning content that violates Pinterest's terms of service, it's best to keep your opinion to yourself. Just as you have your own space on Pinterest to express yourself and your brand, other pinners have the same right. Always be respectful in your comments and conversations on Pinterest. This is a place to showcase inspiration, not bash what other users love.

Rule 2: Be Authentic

According to Pinterest, "Pinterest is an expression of who you are. We think being authentic to who you are is more important than getting lots of followers. Being authentic will make Pinterest a better place long-term." In other words, maintain your Pinterest integrity by staying true to who your company is and accurately representing what you're about, the services you provide, and the products you produce.

Falsifying any aspect of your company might gain you some extra followers in the short run. But in the long term, being anything but completely authentic on Pinterest is a bad idea and will ultimately do nothing but damage your brand.

Rule 3: Credit Your Sources

Pins are most useful and effective when they link back to the original source rather than a source like an image search engine (e.g., Google Images) or a blog entry. Pinterest encourages users to "leave a comment so that the pinner can update the source when they have noticed that an image is sourced incorrectly." Unfortunately, this is a very important rule many well-intentioned pinners break all the time.

Most pinners use the Pin It bookmarklet as soon as they come across something they find online that's pinworthy. Because pinning is such a quick and easy thing to do, most pinners neglect to do their due diligence by tracing that pin back to its original source.

Avoid breaking this rule by taking the time to find a pin's original source. This will create a better experience for those who follow you. And just as Pinterest recommends, let pinners know when something they've pinned links to an incorrect source. If you want to be a superhelpful pinner—and earn some great Pinterest karma—leave a comment including the proper link. You may even earn yourself a new follower.

The Least You Need to Know

- Being highly selective when choosing whom to follow is a great strategic approach.
- When building your following list, first look to your established contacts from your existing social media platforms and your company's mailing list.
- Many Pinterest users look to their favorite pinners or brand's "following" list to inform them on whom to follow. Be sure yours is worth other users' interest.
- Grab other pinners' attention by engaging with them through comments, via repins, and by using the @ mention—you might even get some new followers from your efforts.
- Building a large following on Pinterest takes time and dedication. Consistently pin high-quality content, and like-minded pinners eventually will find and follow you.
- Abiding by Pinterest's top three etiquette rules is important to having a successful and positive Pinterest experience.

Collaborating for Success

In This Chapter

- One board, many pinners
- Creating a virtual neighborhood
- Engaging your followers
- Getting advocates to promote your brand
- Should you pay for pins?
- Working with pinners from other companies

We explained the practical side of creating collaborative boards in Chapter 3. So in this chapter, we want to present the tactical side of collaborative boards. We show you the type of content that works best on collaborative boards and help you identify the right collaborators, both inside and outside of your company.

We also give you ideas for creative collaboration, such as contests and pin exchanges with other businesses that have complementary services or products. At the end of the chapter, we explain the difference between brand advocates and sponsored pins, and the advantages (and occasional disadvantages) of each type of relationship.

Creating and Using Collaborative Boards

The first place to look for collaborators is within your company. You may be surprised to learn how many people are using Pinterest, and that means more eyes on the lookout for great images to pin. Talk to people you know in different departments or in other locations to come up with ways they can support the boards and presence you want to create. Next, consider contractors and consultants who work with you. Outside collaborators will be key if you run a small, or one-person, business.

There are two important benefits to collaboration:

- You become visible to the followers of your collaborators, possibly increasing your reach.
- Your pins come from a variety of sources, which makes your boards less self-promotional.

All the Chronicle Books boards are collaborative boards. Contributors include editors, writers, designers, and community managers who work for or with Chronicle Books, and each has his or her own Pinterest account. We find their "Spotted!" board particularly effective because it shows Chronicle Book projects that have been seen—that is, *spotted*—on other websites or in bookstores that display their books. For example, Chronicle Books publishes a paint-by-number kit, and one of the pins shows a painting from the kit.

PIN TIP

Collaborative boards are identified by a symbol that looks like three heads: **᎒᎒᎒**. Look for it next to the number of pins in the board.

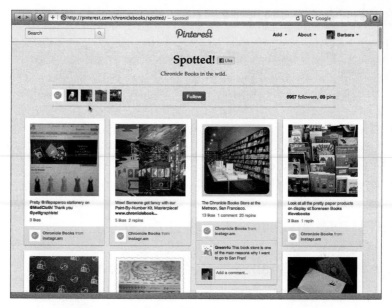

Invite co-workers in other departments to contribute to your boards.
(Chronicle Books)

Connecting with Your Community

We've said it already, but it bears repeating: the success of your marketing efforts is linked to the relationships you develop with your present and future clients. Creating collaborative boards gives you a chance to get to know your clients and makes them feel emotionally invested in your brand.

After creating collaborative efforts with other people within your company, the next group you want to collaborate with is your Pinterest community. Collaboration can help your presence grow exponentially, and collaborating with carefully chosen pinners helps you reach the appropriate audience.

Your Pinterest presence is measured by several factors, including these:

- The number of followers you have
- The number of boards you have and pins you post
- The number of repins your pins generate

With a coordinated marketing effort, you'll see your presence grow on a steady basis.

Now let's look at how collaborative boards can work for a service-based business-to-business company and for a business-to-consumer product-based company.

Business-to-Business Collaboration

If your client already uses Pinterest, terrific! There won't be a big learning curve, and collaboration can come about quite naturally. One or two boards focused on the project you're working on allows the client to post things he likes and allows you to post things you're working on. This benefits the client at hand and is an innovative way to work together. It also shows your potential clients your work in progress, which is a great testament to your work style and ethic. (Obviously, you won't exhibit sensitive information on the shared board.)

If the client isn't familiar with Pinterest, take the opportunity to introduce the platform. This reinforces the fact that you're current on the latest technology and marketing methods and may provide a tool for your client to market his product or service as well. Let's say you're a shoe manufacturer and sell your shoes wholesale to retailers. Although the retailer is your client, the retailer's clients (consumers) are also indirectly your clients. Collaboration benefits both of you.

PIN TIP

You also want to follow clients who are on Pinterest to stay informed on their activities and interests and to boost this Pinterest presence.

Business-to-Consumer Collaboration

The most obvious business-to-consumer collaboration is asking customers to pin images of your product or service on your boards and their boards as well. These pins could be photos they take of themselves or that they feel emulate a lifestyle that resonates with your product or service. You can also request content that relates to your offering.

An example of an enterprising collaboration is the "Small Kitchen College Recipes" board on the Big Girls, Small Kitchen profile. The two young women who started the Big Girls, Small Kitchen blog, which provides cooking lessons and recipes for college students and recent grads, use Pinterest to showcase their advice. The "Small Kitchen College Recipes" board is a collaborative board. The Big Girls, Small Kitchen followers are likely to purchase a copy of *In the Small Kitchen*, the book that has resulted from their blogging efforts.

Having more than one collaborator helps fill your boards with pins and is a promotional opportunity for the contributors, too.

(top row: Lucy Dana, Will Levitt, Priya Krishna, Candice Allouch; second row: Julie Sophonpanich, Jen Cantin, Sarah Buchanan, Candice Allouch)

Create themed boards to conduct visual focus groups with your customers. Here are just a few ideas of how this can work:

- Pin prototypes of future products, and ask for comments.
- Pin an infographic of a survey that links to a survey website.
- Make your customers part of your product development team by asking them to pin desires they'd like your product to satisfy.

Running Contests

Promotional contests have always been part of great brand marketing strategies, and as more brands start to get an understanding of how Pinterest works, they start to get creative with how to run Pinterest contests. At the moment, there isn't a lot of data available to gauge the impact of contests across Pinterest, but it seems to certainly be a concept worth exploring.

Country Living magazine runs frequent contests on its website, countryliving.com, for lovely editorial products. As a way to bring attention to the contests running on the website, *Country Living* magazine has started to pin these prizes to a Pinterest board called "Win This!" with the instruction "Go to countryliving.com/win and enter for a chance to win these great prizes!" in the board description.

For *Country Living* magazine, Pinterest a great place to announce exciting contests and an effective way to divert traffic from Pinterest to its website. And as its followers repin the beautiful contest products that are up for grabs, they're informing all their followers of the frequent contests *Country Living* conducts. If we weren't already following *Country Living* magazine on Pinterest, announcements of its contests over Pinterest would definitely make us new followers.

In February 2012, the popular online fashion publication Style Bistro conducted a unique contest of its own on Pinterest. In an effort to publicize its superb coverage of New York Fashion Week, Style Bistro created a contest asking readers to create a board called "Fashion Week Favorites." Then contestants were told to head over to Style Bistro's extensive collection of Fashion Week photos and complete contest boards by pinning their favorite Fashion Week looks. To submit contest boards, Style Bistro contestants were directed to Style Bistro's Facebook page, where they had to post a link to their Pinterest contest board.

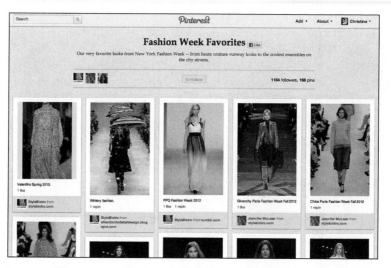

Use contests to invite your followers to collaborate on your boards.

With a prize of $250 worth of editor-picked beauty products, Style Bistro followers had an excellent incentive to join the contest. And for those readers who wanted to participate but weren't yet on Pinterest, Style Bistro offered invites to the site. For Style Bistro, it was a smart way to draw readers' attention to its Pinterest presence, spread content from its site onto Pinterest by asking participants to pin a lot of content it made available, and promote its Pinterest page to its established followers. No doubt, it was able to pick up a ton of new followers and create a lot of excitement around its Pinterest account.

Finally, because we've been noticing quite a few "pin it to win it" pins floating around Pinterest, we thought we'd mention this type of quick and easy Pinterest contest several brands have been experimenting with.

Country Outfitter, a retail store that specializes on fashionable western wear for men and women, ran a Pinterest contest in April 2012. It involved two simple "pin it to win it" steps. On its blog, Country Outfitter created a "pin it to win it" ad that explained the contest rules. To enter the contest, followers had to pin the image it created from its blog onto Pinterest, along with a pair of boots from its website. All the contest required was two simple pins to enter.

MARKETING MIX-UP

For now, Pinterest hasn't released any rules or legal guidelines for promoting contests on the site (whereas Facebook prohibits the use of any of its native applications for contest purposes). Be sure you stay up to date on the Pinterest terms of use.

Use print and web advertising to promote contests you run on Pinterest.

This simple contest was a great way for Country Outfitter to spread the word about its brand to the followers of each and every one of its customers who entered. The contest pins themselves were also a smart way to divert traffic from Pinterest back to its website and blog. Given just how simple Country Outfitter made its Pinterest contest, we're sure it had a lot of customers enter and, as a result, spread awareness of its brand across thousands of Pinterest users.

> **VERY PINTERESTING!**
>
> What you learn about a person through their collections is true to who they are.
>
> —Pinterest founder Ben Silbermann at the L2 Innovation Forum, 2010

Soliciting Brand Advocates

Traditional advertising relied on showing a celebrity—or at the very least someone very attractive—using a product or service, conveying the idea that if consumers use that product or service, some of the celebrity or beauty will rub off on them. Today, consumers are more savvy … and perhaps more cynical. It's not enough anymore to see a celebrity use a product; that celebrity has to instill trust. That same kind of trust is built with Pinterest pinners. When one pinner follows another pinner, an implicit trust begins to build to the point that the follower looks to the pinner for advice.

Today, bloggers, vloggers, and now pinners are tastemakers, and followers want to emulate and live the lifestyle of those they follow. Essentially, the tastemaker has replaced the celebrity endorsement. To take advantage of this trend, you want tastemakers to be your *brand advocates.*

> **DEFINITION**
>
> **Brand advocates** are people—or pinners, in our case—who recommend products and services without being paid to do so. They must be trustworthy and have a high level of online influence, which translates into a high number of friends and followers on social networks and active engagement.

To identify brand advocates on Pinterest, look for pinners who follow you who have the following characteristics:

- They frequently repin your pins.
- They have a high number of followers.
- They also have a strong presence on other social networks—more than 500 friends on Facebook, for example.
- They're actively engaged in Pinterest.

After you identify a few potential brand advocates, contact them by email and begin to establish a relationship. It's likely they not only enjoy your product or service but have a personal interest in it as well, making them a good source for information about improving your offerings.

You also may want to seed upcoming products to these advocates before the official release to coordinate "buzz" with the product or service launch.

A study conducted by Zuberance about brand advocacy found that brand advocates make recommendations because of a good experience and a desire to help others. These motives account for the authenticity and trustworthiness of a good brand advocate.

Sponsored Pin Relationships

Now that companies have a sense for how powerful the reach of a pin can be, sponsored pin relationships are starting to be presented to those users who have the ability to reach a lot of users with their pins. Some brands offer incentives to their established brand advocates, while other brands reach out to power pinners with large followings.

A *sponsored pin* is a paid-for pin pinned by a power pinner on behalf of a brand. Essentially, that pin is a paid-for ad and acts in the same way a sponsored post on a blog would work.

DEFINITION

A **sponsored pin** is a paid-for pin presented by an influential Pinterest user for a brand in an effort to increase brand awareness and potentially drive traffic and sales for that brand.

Some brands are beginning to approach influential power pinners on their own and offer some kind of monetary payment in exchange for a pin or a series of pins. In other cases, agencies are connecting influential pinners to complementary brands they have an affiliate relationship with to broker these types of sponsored pin relationships for both parties.

Recently, there's been quite a bit of controversy around sponsored pin relationships because of the lack of transparency around which pins have been paid for and which were unsolicited pinned. Even influential pinners have started to come under fire for not making it clear if a pin has been sponsored. Many are starting to change their sponsored pin approach in order to make these relationships known.

Sponsored pin relationships can be a positive thing between influential pinners and brands, but it seems that transparency about the relationship—and notification that a pin has been paid for—is important. If your company decides to sponsor a series of pins or a single pin with an influential user, be sure to indicate that pins you've requested were sponsored.

Cross-Promotional Pinning

Cross-promotional pinning is a type of collaboration we think your business could benefit from.

There are two types of cross-promotional pinning. The first is when many like-minded pinners pin on a larger site, such as artisans contributing to Etsy boards. The second type is when two businesses with complementary products or services contribute to each other's boards. In both cases, the benefit is mutual because all parties involved increase their followers and pin potential.

The Least You Need to Know

- Identify pinners inside and outside your company to collaborate with.

- Use collaborative boards to hold image-driven conversations with clients about projects.

- Promotional contests on Pinterest can be fun and extremely successful.

- Establish a relationship with brand advocates who will recommend your product or service.

- Sponsored pin relationships on Pinterest can be controversial if both the brand and the pinner are not upfront about the fact that a pin has been paid for. Transparency is key.

- Look for new ways to collaborate with like-minded pinners and complementary businesses.

Taking Pinterest Further

As a new Pinterest expert, you now have all the tools, tips, and best practice knowledge to launch a successful Pinterest account for your business. But to be a true Pinterest expert and utilize this social media platform to its fullest, you'll need to understand how to take Pinterest one step further. That means knowing what feedback is important and how to analyze that critical information.

Chapter 13 covers the different ways to evaluate how effective your Pinterest efforts are by analyzing your site statistics, and by reviewing the different types of feedback you'll experience on Pinterest. Chapter 14 helps you take a closer look at your website and/or blog through Pinterest lenses to determine whether or not your brand is pinworthy to others. And last but certainly not least, Chapter 15 sends you on your way to maintaining your brand presence and influence on this here-to-stay social media platform.

Evaluating Your Pinterest Effectiveness

Chapter 13

In This Chapter

- Tracking pins and following numbers
- Keeping the conversation open
- Gathering data from your Pinterest followers
- Using pins to ask questions
- Interpreting the repins

If you manage other social network accounts or your company's website or blog, you probably track how many times your website or blog is viewed and when it receives the most views. (And if you don't, you should.) Time is money, and you want to use both wisely. You want to know what kind of return you're getting for the time you invest in your online marketing efforts.

Many tools are available for tracking this information. Some, like those connected with Google's Blogger, are built into the product. Others are run by third parties such as Klout or RJMetrics. At the time of writing, Pinterest doesn't have built-in analytics, although several Pinterest-specific analytics companies are active and Pinterest activity can be tracked by the companies that also track Facebook, Twitter, and other social networks.

We open this chapter by outlining the types of analytics that help you measure the success of your Pinterest marketing efforts. We introduce you to some of the companies that offer analytic services and then show you a couple ways to solicit and interpret direct feedback from followers. The second half of the chapter gives you some ideas for conducting research on Pinterest to gain information about your clients and about the effectiveness of your Pinterest presence.

Site Statistics and Referral Traffic

When you look at your Pinterest profile, you can easily see the number of boards and pins you have. But there are three other pieces of information that are crucial for you to know:

- Which of your pins are most popular, measured by the number of times they've been repinned
- Which boards are the most followed
- What images from your website or blog have been pinned by pinners other than yourself

Repins are important because they increase your presence across Pinterest and are one of the most countable items used to calculate your influence. You can scroll through the Pins view on your profile page to see which pins have been repinned and how often, but if you have a lot of pins, this will take you a big chunk of time. Luckily, analytics provide this information much quicker and easier.

Likewise, to see how many followers each board has, you have to open each one individually—an activity that's both tedious and time-consuming. Analytics can provide an overview of how many followers each board has, and if you combine that information with the number of repins, you begin to get a picture of which aspects of your business are most popular.

> **PIN TIP**
>
> Creating boards that represent different parts of your business and then analyzing which boards receive the best response gives you an indicator about which parts of your business customers respond to most.

Are You Being Pinned?

Knowing what content has been pinned from your website helps you decide the types of images you want to post in the future. Remember, when an image is posted from your website and someone clicks through the pin, they reach your website—and that's always a good thing. Notice that you can see who's pinning your images. If you find the same pinner frequently pinning from your website, you've identified a voluntary brand advocate. (Remember, we talked about those in Chapter 12.)

We noticed images from Anthropologie.com are frequently pinned, and one thing we found interesting was that none of the Anthropologie boards are collaborative, yet on any given day, you find at least a handful of Anthropologie pins that aren't from Anthropologie. Clearly, it has a popular product that speaks to a large audience, but it also provides a lot of pinnable content on its website—a tactic your brand should strive to emulate. Out of curiosity, we did a search on images that show up from Barbara's blog, Honeybees and Olive Trees, and this is the result.

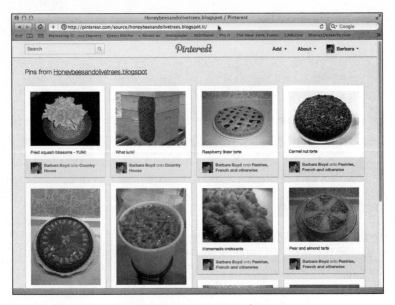

To find out who's been pinning images from your website, go to pinterest.com/source/yourwebsiteURL, without http:// *or* www.

Using Analytics to Count Repins and Followers

With the success of Pinterest, several Pinterest-specific analytics providers have shown up next to broad-based social media analytics providers. Following is a list of some analytics providers, most of which provide other services as well. We neither endorse nor criticize any of them and want only to give you a head start in finding one that's right for you. Please read their offerings carefully to see which one suits your business needs. Most offer a trial service, so we suggest you try before you buy.

- Google Analytics: google.com/analytics
- HubSpot: hubspot.com
- Klout: klout.com
- Pinerly: pinerly.com

- Pinpuff: pinpuff.com
- PinReach Analytics: pinreach.com
- Pintics: signup.pintics.com
- RJMetrics: rjmetrics.com

For those of you unfamiliar with analytics, here's an example of analytics done on Christine's Pinterest account. You can see that her score has increased in the last week and her most popular pins have held steady. Clicking on the **Boards** tab reveals information for each board, such as the number of repins, followers, and comments. Clicking the **Pins** tab shows thumbnail images of Christine's most popular pins, or those that have been repinned the most. Lastly, **Influential Followers** shows the pinners who have a high PinReach score and follow Christine.

Analytics sites can tell you which of your pins are most popular, how many followers you have for each board, and how influential you are on Pinterest.
(© 2012 PinReach, LLC)

PIN TIP

PinReach lets you see pinners with the highest PinReach score, even without setting up a profile, which can help you find collaborators for your boards.

PinReach is a Pinterest-specific analytics provider. Companies like HubSpot, RJMetrics, and Google Analytics look at all your online marketing efforts to determine which are most effective in converting visits to a website or social media site to customers. For example, they track the percentage of people who viewed your boards on Pinterest and then visited your website to purchase something, as compared to those who visited your Facebook page and then went to your website to make a purchase.

Responding to and Soliciting Comments

Direct feedback on your pins is great, although read it with a discerning eye. Comments can be negative or positive. Oftentimes, negative comments are from people who don't understand how Pinterest works. The comments tend to be "Why do I keep seeing these pins I didn't request?" or "Who is this person?"

The polite thing to do is explain that when you set up a Pinterest account, Pinterest automatically sets you up to follow fellow pinners in the categories you checked that you were interested in. You can also say that to "unfollow," the other user can click the **Unfollow** button at the top of a board.

MARKETING MIX-UP

Every time you make or respond to a comment, you have a chance to reinforce your brand. Remember the golden rules: be nice and say please and thank you.

Negative comments directed at your product or service must be responded to with professionalism and clarity. Your best tactic is to address the issue as simply as possible in the comments area so other pinners see you are responsive to your clients. If the issue is very personal or specific to the pinner who commented, get in touch with him directly, ask for clarification, and remedy the issue immediately.

Negative comments are a huge help in improving your business, but positive comments also do a few things:

- Build your reputation, especially if the comment is from a power pinner or brand advocate
- Solicit a longer engagement between followers and the specific pin, since they hang around to read the comments
- Let you know what you're doing right
- Make you feel warm and fuzzy, brighten your day, and boost your business confidence

One comment often spurs a conversation. It's hard to say what pins will generate a comment, although the description you write on the pin can help. Simple yet enthusiastic prompts like, "We love this new spring color. And you?" or "We're thrilled to offer *a new service/product*" are more likely to trigger a comment than a dry, sedate description.

Of course, you can always specifically ask followers to leave a comment with their opinion about the pin.

Pinterest as a Focus Group

Any time one of your pins is repinned, receives a like, or gets a comment, you are receiving feedback from a potential customer. The information you cull from these types of feedback can be thought of as an informal *focus group*. We wrote about comments in the previous section, so let's look at the other two forms of feedback.

Repinning states "I like this so much I want to tell other people about it" and "I want to include it in one of my collections." It's almost the equivalent of saying "I love it!" Repins are a clear indication of what you're doing right.

A like is more vague, as if the customer was saying "I'm just looking." We talked about how you can use the Like feature to tag a pin for later consideration, and we're certainly not the only pinners to do this. A like is free of commitment. That's not to say it's negative, but the pin doesn't resonate enough to solicit a repin. If you have a pin with only likes and no repins, compare it to a pin that's been repinned frequently, and try to determine the difference.

Your information gathering doesn't have to be passive. When you want to sound out your customers, in addition to asking for feedback on a specific pin, as we mentioned earlier, create a board called "Tell Us What You Think" or "We Want to Hear from You." Pin a mix of images that can be simply liked or commented on, or create graphics of specific questions and ask for a response in the comments.

Country Living magazine uses its boards to get feedback from its readers and at the same time create a relationship with them. Its boards are a visual conversation with essential words exchanged and many images that convey feeling and connection. To create the Your Favorite CL Rooms board (pinterest.com/countryliving/your-favorite-cl-rooms), *Country Living* uses pinterest.com/source/countryliving.com to find images that have been pinned from its website. It then repins those images to this board and asks the original pinners to comment if they find their image there. *Country Living* adds comments, and that's often enough to spark responses, leading to a longer conversation.

> **VERY PINTERESTING!**
>
> More comments translate into more engagement, and that leads to stronger brand recognition and often results in more customers.

Conducting Surveys

Surveys can be an effective way to obtain information about your current or potential clients, although there's quite a bit of work involved before, during, and after a survey.

Initially, you have to think about what kind of information you want to learn about your present or future customers. Are you looking for simple demographics to get an idea of the size of the market? Do you want to know specifically what your customers think of your products or services? And if so, do you want their opinions based on what they see in advertising or based on their actual experience in using the product? Do you want to collect data and personal information so you can add the person to your mailing list? You're probably beginning to get the picture.

After you define the type of data you want to gather, you have to formulate questions that will solicit that information. Your questions need to be simple, ideally quantifiable with a number, appropriate to the audience, and not open to false interpretation.

The answers should be quantifiable so you can tally the responses you receive. Providing a scale of 0 to 9 or 1 to 5, for example, that correlates with the question leads to results you can average.

The data entry and tallying is no small feat, and then you must interpret the data. If you are a small business, we suggest you turn to an expert to conduct formal surveys. Online survey companies such as SurveyMonkey do a fine job creating a survey and tallying the results. If you feel you need more information about your customers to better your business, paying for such a service is probably money well spent. You can use a pin or board to drive followers from Pinterest to the survey site.

> **MARKETING MIX-UP**
>
> Unfortunately, Pinterest was the target of a series of spams that used enticing surveys ($100 of free makeup or a luxury handbag just for answering a few questions) to lure people to fake websites and use information gathered in potentially criminal ways. For now, the Pinterest community remains suspect of other surveying activities, so you may have to wait a while to conduct a survey on Pinterest.

Understanding Visual Feedback

Pinterest is a conversation conducted in images between you and your current and future customers or clients. You tell your brand story and convey your vision, ideals, products, and services across your Pinterest boards and the pins you place on them. Likewise, you receive visual feedback.

Here's an interesting, and quite simple, exercise you can do to see which of your pins are really having an impact. In the Pinterest search field, type your company name and click the **Pins** tab. Notice how many pins of the same image appear. If you have a product line, the resulting visual can be a crystal ball looking at your upcoming seasonal sales. Information like this provides an incredible tool for short-term projections that's even more useful than the analytics and surveys combined.

This is where Pinterest can give you data no other social media platform can. Seeing which pins were repinned the most gives you immediate visual feedback of what part of your business is having the biggest impact and where your future efforts may best be placed.

The Least You Need to Know

- Use marketing analytics to determine the effectiveness of your online presence on Pinterest and elsewhere.
- Prompt comments with questions and enthusiastic pin descriptions.

- Gather information about your customers from likes, repins, and comments.
- Conduct informal surveys by asking your followers to communicate with pins.
- Use visual feedback to make short-term marketing decisions.

Making Your Brand Pinnable

In This Chapter

- How Pinterest-friendly is your website?
- Optimizing your blog for Pinterest
- Making your images pinworthy

Throughout the chapters of this book, we've explained what Pinterest is all about and provided solid strategic tips on how to become a respected and followed brand. We've shared the ins and outs of creating interesting and brand-relevant topic boards, given you tips on creating Pinteresting copy, and pointed you in the direction of some of the best places online to find stellar pinworthy images.

Now that you're a pinning pro, it's time to look at the way your company relates with Pinterest on the *other* side of pinning. How do you make your brand's website and blog places pinners searching for content want to pin from? Instinctively, you may have been asking yourself this question all along. As we've taken you through the process of what to look for when you're searching for content to pin, we're sure you've wondered if your own website is pinworthy. If the thought hadn't crossed your mind until now, don't worry! We've kept your mind full of enough information to process so far.

Now it's time to turn the tables and learn how to make your brand's website and blog a place worthy of being pinned from, complete with beautiful pinworthy images that will attract pinners.

Making Your Website and Blog Pinterest Friendly

According to data released by Experian Marketing Services, in April 2012, Pinterest was the third most popular social site on the internet behind Facebook and Twitter. It's just as important to have your company pinned by pinners as it is to have them mention and like you on Facebook or tweet about you on Twitter. That means it's time to make your website highly pinnable.

Evaluating Your Website

When you begin to examine your website and/or blog to see if it's Pinterest friendly, you're going to want to ask yourself some questions.

For example, does your company's website contain a lot of visual material? This is one of the most important questions you'll need to consider and one you'll likely want to answer first. If the answer is "no," you've probably realized your website isn't somewhere pinners can (or want to) pin from.

Is your company's website Flash based? If so, you might be out of luck. Flash websites are not optimized for pinning on Pinterest because the Pin It bookmarklet won't work for Flash-based sites.

If your company's website does contain a lot of images that can be pinned, what's the quality of those images? Do they make a high visual impact? Are they appealing or interesting?

If you have a blog, do you have a corresponding image with every post? If so, are those images engaging?

Keeping in mind the quality of images you search for when you're pinning, if you weren't connected to your company, would you want to pin from your website? That might be a tough question to ask yourself, but it's an important one. If the answer is "no," you've got some work to do to make your site pinworthy.

Are Your Website Images Pinnable?

Content Science is an award-winning consultant firm that works with Fortune 500 companies, startups, institutions, and government agencies on digital content strategy. Savvy as it is, it understood that it was just as important that visitors could pin from its site as it was to establish a brand profile on Pinterest. Content Science recently evaluated its website to ensure it was up to joining the Pinterest party.

The first place the smart folks at Content Science went to test its website's pinnability was the home page. A quick Pin It test proved unsuccessful. As you can see from the following figure, no images were detected on this page, even though several images appear there.

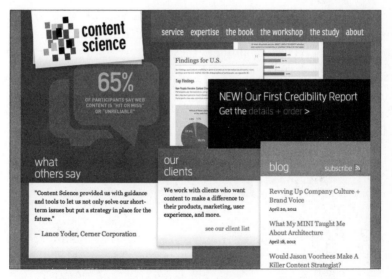

If your website isn't pinnable, visitors who try to pin your images will receive an error message.

Curious about why the images on the home page weren't pinnable, the Content Science crew did a little investigating and found that the logo and other home page images were programmed using CSS (cascading style sheets) background images. CSS background images are useful for constructing websites, but they hide the data Pinterest searches for when identifying images for pinning. Content Science eventually figured out a solution to the problem.

MARKETING MIX-UP

Website images programmed using CSS background images have the data required for pinning hidden. If you want to ensure the images on your website are pinnable, you may want to think twice about using CSS.

As mentioned earlier in this chapter, images from Flash-based websites aren't pinnable. Flash websites can be great for online engagement, but if your company has a Flash-based website, you're missing out on the opportunity to have your content pinned. Making major changes to your Flash website in order to optimize it for pinning could be a costly endeavor, but now that Pinterest is the third most popular social site on the internet, it's one you might want to consider.

Several large consumer and top global brands like Adidas, Harley-Davidson, Pepsi, Loréal, Hyundai, and Cartier love using Flash on their websites. As eye-catching as these sites are, they're missing the Pinterest boat. If you're keen on having content from your company's website pinned onto Pinterest, you may want to make some big adjustments so pinners searching for content don't see error messages when they try to pin images from your website.

By having a Flash-based website, Cartier has missed the opportunity to have pinners showcase their products on Pinterest.

Evaluating Your Blog

Making your blog pinnable is also highly important and should be a priority—particularly if your blog is your business! We've found that blogs are a natural source of great pin content because most bloggers incorporate a lot of complementary images and videos. But we've also come across quite a few blogs that could certainly step up their pinnability factor. Here are a couple questions you should ask yourself when evaluating how pinnable your blog is:

Do you include high-quality images with each and every blog post? If not, it's time you start considering adding a high-quality image to complement your posts. A lot of pinners enjoy pinning interesting articles they find online if the article provides them with some way of making itself pinnable. If there's an image to go along with the articles you post, pinning won't be a problem!

But as always, we must emphasize using high-quality images. The better your images, the better your pinnability.

If you post videos on your blog, are they being embedded from YouTube or Vimeo? If your videos aren't being embedded into your blog, pinners won't be able to pin them from your blog, or anywhere else for that matter.

Doing It Right

Katie Armour is a blogger and entrepreneur who knows how to make a beautiful splash on the internet. Her highly pinnable blog, The Neo-Traditionalist, is a popular spot for pinners looking for fashion and lifestyle inspiration. Katie puts forth the type of content that's popular among female pinners, but more importantly, she uses single, high-quality standalone images in each and every one of her stylized posts. Katie also likes to use large images in her post that are perfect for grabbing attention on Pinterest. Take a look at the image sizes posted on The Neo-Traditionalist; they are all 500 pixels wide.

The Neo-Traditionalist by Katie Armour is a highly pinnable blog because of its stunning imagery and strong content.

Images this large make for some of the most visually effective pins. The pins appear to be the same general size when you look at them on the main grid view, but when you click a pin, if the image size pinned was large (above 300 pixels), the pin gives pinners a great and detailed view of the content from your site.

The Neo-Traditionalist's main pinnable images are all quite large, ranging from about 600 pixels to 800 pixels.

PIN TIP

Learning by example is always a great approach to take when optimizing your website. Find blogs and websites you admire when you're in the process of making your site more pinnable, and follow their lead.

Let's look at a couple examples of images Christine has pinned so you can see for yourself.

The first example is a product she pinned. She loved the laptop case but was disappointed in the size of the image. It was difficult for other pinners to tell just how great the product was, and the small size of the image kept this particular pin from being liked and repinned as many times as she would have expected.

Christine Martinez
Pinned 7 weeks ago via **pinmarklet**

⇅ Repin   Edit   From ahalife.com

Retro Denim 13-inch Laptop Case by Thomas Paul. I've seen the canvas version but I love the more durable denim option.

Pinned via **pinmarklet**

The laptop case image is quite small, leaving a lot of white space around the image itself.

On the contrary, the following pin, with a width size of 500 pixels, gives Pinterest users a large and attractive view of this living room interior inspiration shot. It's almost like looking at this picture in a magazine. Yes, the photograph itself is beautiful, which makes it highly repinnable. But had this image been small, let's say under 200 pixels, it wouldn't have had nearly the same kind of impact.

The image of this living room is so large, it takes up the majority of the pin view.

Currently, Pinterest allows for image sizes to be up to 600 pixels wide. Take advantage of this! Make your blog highly pinnable by posting large images.

Pinterest is a lot less restrictive when it comes to the image length. For maximum pin impact, pin images with a large pixel length. They really stand out when you're looking at pins in the grid view.

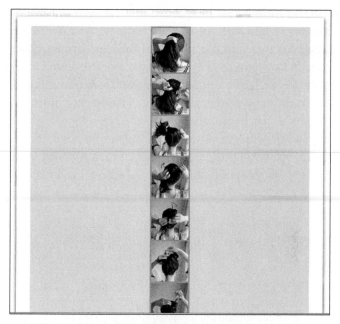

This tutorial pin has taken advantage of the less restrictive pin length. You can see here how long this pin is relative to most.

Creating High-Quality Images for Pinterest

Now that you've ensured your website is pinnable, or know what you need to do to make it pinnable, it's time to focus your energy on creating high-quality images pinners will want to pin and share.

If you're a large company, you probably have go-to photographers and a creative team to put together stellar shots. But if you're a small business without a lot of cash to spend on hiring stylists and photographers, you can still create the illusion that you do. That's one of the great parts about the internet!

If you've spent a lot of time on Pinterest admiring the beautiful images some pinners pin, you may feel a bit intimidated as a small business owner. You might be wondering, *How on earth am I going to be able to create images that look like something you'd see in a magazine?* Based on personal experience as a small business owner, Christine knows exactly how you feel. She was once that entrepreneur researching all her favorite ecommerce sites and wondering how she was going to create anything that came close to the stunning photos she admired with such a limited budget. We're happy to report it wasn't impossible. All it took was a willingness to get creative and work hard. With no photography experience whatsoever, Christine took the following photograph for her website in her kitchen.

Teapot with a cold
Pinned via web

Christine shot this "Teapot with a Cold" in her kitchen using only natural sunlight.

To truly capture the teapot, she shot it very close up. To highlight its sweet nature and subtle colors, she bought some complementary pink fabric to use as a tablecloth and used her buttery walls as a backdrop. Then she added the spoon and cup to give the teapot some scale.

It's great to have a vision in mind of the types of photographs you want to create for your business. Researching your favorite websites and spending time finding your favorite photo inspiration pins on Pinterest will help guide you through this creative endeavor. In fact, you should create a Pinterest board called "Website Photography Inspiration" for some helpful visual feedback.

Once you have a vision in mind, it's helpful to break down any big tasks into easy-to-follow steps. Here's the step-by-step process Christine went through to create beautiful images for her website and blog.

If you're going to be photographing the images for your company's website or blog yourself, it's wise to invest in a quality digital camera. We're particularly fond of SLR cameras over most point-and-shoot options because their technical capabilities far exceed those of a simple point-and-shoot. Professional photographers almost always use SLR cameras.

When taking high-quality photographs, it's important to be able to manually set aperture priority, shutter priority, ISO range, and shutter lag or have the option to use a variety of lenses. If these words are completely foreign to you, don't worry! Plenty of great YouTube tutorials can walk you through using an SLR. At this point, the most important thing to know is that SLR cameras can take visually stunning photos most point-and-shoot cameras could never capture.

Having the right photo accessories to complete the job is also im- portant to creating perfect photos. We highly recommend covering the basics, like a tripod and a white box (if you're a retailer and would like to shoot studiolike white background images). These types of product images look great on Pinterest.

VERY PINTERESTING!

White boxes aren't terribly expensive for the most part, but you can easily make your own. In fact, after doing a quick Pinterest search for "DIY white box," we found some helpful tutorials.

Christine took this white-boxed product photo in her own white box she set up in her backyard. She opted to use natural light.

Photo-editing software is a key element in creating gorgeous, pinworthy photos. Photoshop, Pixelmator, Acorn, and Photo Studio are all great options. It takes a bit of knowledge to be able to use these programs, so be sure to watch tutorials, take a class, or ask a friend or colleague who knows how to use one of these programs well. Christine relies pretty heavily on Photoshop to brighten images and touch up imperfections. Even with a basic knowledge of how to use the software, she was able to create beautiful images.

Christine has consulted with quite a few small business owners over the past few years, and she always advises them to allocate a significant amount of their resources to creating a beautiful website with great photography.

We don't believe you need all the bells some websites incorporate that can end up costing you a lot of money. A simple and visually beautiful space where internet users will want to spend some time exploring—and now, pinning!—is all you need. For proof, just take a look at the profound impact Pinterest is having on how we visually experience the internet. If you want your business to make its way through Pinterest, it's time to step up your visual game.

The Least You Need to Know

- Incorporating high-quality and visually stunning images into your company's website and blog is a huge step in the right direction of making your website highly pinnable.

- Flash-based websites and images programmed using CSS (cascading style sheets) are not pinnable by Pinterest, so avoid using these options on your sites (and consider updating and removing if you do).

- If your company posts videos on your website and/or blog, be sure the videos are being embedded from YouTube or Vimeo.

- Using large images on your website and blog will make a greater impact when they're later pinned onto Pinterest, and larger and more impactful images have a greater chance of being repinned.

- Creating vibrant, high-quality images for your site will make all the difference in whether your site content gets pinned.

Maintaining Your Pinterest Presence

Chapter 15

In This Chapter

- Using Pinterest to announce company news
- Creating memorable boards
- Investing the time to see success
- Looking at your Pinterest future

Like everything in life, your company is going to go through several changes over time, particularly if you're a small business just starting out. Oftentimes, it takes several years of trial and error to find your voice and identity as a brand. And even when you think you've found your brand's sweet spot, it's important to keep your brand evolving over time to reflect the industry and social changes constantly in play. In fact, learning how to use a social media platform like Pinterest to market your business reflects a big change in the way you've started to market online!

In this final chapter, we take you through the process of reflecting your company changes on Pinterest by producing content that's fresh and current, and by keeping your business eyes peeled for trends occurring on the Pinterest. But as you'll discover, the biggest take-home message here is being persistent with your marketing efforts. After all, success within social media doesn't happen overnight.

Reflecting Company Changes on Pinterest

All businesses, both small and large, typically go through a series of major changes over the course of their life span. Pinterest itself has undergone a few big redesigns, the additions of new features, and a whole lot of trial and error in its short existence. It'll be amazing to see where Pinterest is five years from now, what it will look like, and what it will be capable of. We can't wait! So far, we've been big fans of the steps forward Pinterest has taken as a company.

This is what a pin profile looked like when Pinterest started out.

Knowing this, you should expect your business to go through several necessary changes in order to evolve into something bigger and better. Change isn't easy for many people, and oftentimes, you'll lose customers and clients along the way. There will always be those individuals who prefer everything stay the same. But for those customers and clients willing to ride the wave of change with you, it's important to ease them into your company's transitions and keep communication open at all times. Fortunately, interacting and communicating through social media provides companies with a perfect platform to announce new and exciting changes.

Here's what the pin profile looks like at the time of writing.

On Pinterest, announcing new changes to your company can be as simple as adding new boards as changes occur. Not all changes within companies are major, and many of those changes occur seasonally. Retail companies like Bergdorf Goodman do an excellent job of constantly communicating seasonal changes to their multiple product lines, as well as to the hot trends they love at the moment. It will be interesting to see these fashion trends for a brand like Bergdorf Goodman evolve over time, and to be able to look back at the archives of visual information that will accumulate on Pinterest!

If your company undergoes a series of minor changes frequently, create new boards as these changes occur, and let your customer or clients know you've created these new boards. You could let your customers and clients discover these new boards on their own, but creating new boards is a fun and exciting thing to share. And it's the perfect way to entice your customers to come get a glimpse of what's new.

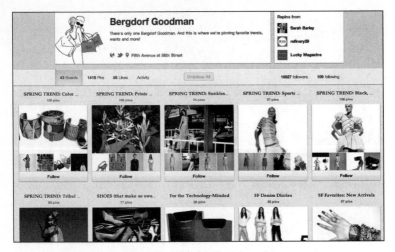

*Announce company changes, both product lines or
personnel changes, on new boards or pins, as Bergdorf
Goodman does on its Pinterest page.*

VERY PINTERESTING!

You may not realize it, but as you add new boards to your company's
Pinterest account to reflect changes occurring with your brand, you're
creating a fascinating visual timeline for your company. Over the years,
your customers and clients will enjoy looking back and seeing how far
your business has come.

Sometimes company changes are major, where brands go through
a process of rebranding themselves to appeal to a new and different
demographic. Several large consumer companies have gone under
large company rebrands over the past decade in order to reflect the
changes within their customer base.

For example, Starbucks has changed its logo four times since opening for business in 1971. Its latest logo, created in 2011, is in line with
a new trend of simplicity in design, one that we're seeing in some of
our favorite products like those being produced by Apple. This type
of bold yet simple design has had a large appeal with a younger and
more savvy consumer audience.

Over time, your pins and boards reflect a timeline of your company's evolution.

Rebranding your company this way could lead to big changes around who you're now marketing to and the type of content you're putting forward to appeal to them. This new branding effort is going to have to be reflected in the way you market on social media platforms like Pinterest, too.

Let's use Starbucks as an example. If someone was creating a Pinterest account around Starbucks in the 1970s, she would put forth content that would appeal to a 30-something coffee drinker who was interested in supporting "mom-and-pop" specialty stores with local followings. This person probably appreciated interacting with her neighbors, woke up early to get in some physical activity like hiking or kayaking, and was most likely well educated.

Over the course of experiencing massive growth and a major brand overhaul, a new Starbucks Pinterest account (that of the 2000s) would appeal to a different type of Starbucks customer—or most likely, several different types of Starbucks customers. Although that original Starbucks customer of the 1970s still exists at the heart of the brand (and Starbucks would still want to pay homage to that customer), it would be critically important to create content for the 20-something startup crowd who meet at Starbucks for the free Wi-Fi and in lieu of having a proper office to interview recruits. It would also have to appeal to the mom who can't wait to drop off her kids at school and grab a cup of coffee at the Starbucks drive-thru.

If you undergo a company rebrand to appeal to a new audience, you need to think about a few things when you're revamping your Pinterest account to reflect those changes. For example, now that you're attempting to reach out to a new audience, you need to create target customer profiles again. These profiles will provide a lot of information you'll need to start putting forth captivating Pinterest pins and boards.

Reaching out to your new target audience is important. Many people might remember your brand as it was and not check back to see it as it exists now. Reach out and pull your new audience in with your new content. Do your Pinterest research, and find those pinners you know will love and appreciate your new changes.

PIN TIP

When you're putting out new content on Pinterest in an attempt to grab a new audience, you have to stay on top of your Pinterest research. You'll be reaching out to a different type of pinner, so go for it! Don't wait around and expect your new audience to find you.

Staying Present by Being Creative

Great marketing is all about being creative, and as you now know, Pinterest is a fantastic place for creative marketing. With image sharing, there are endless possibilities to be discovered and ways to reach and entertain an audience.

One of the best ways to stay present on Pinterest and continue to build a presence is to get creative with how you use the site and the visual content you present. Avid Pinterest users are always on the hunt for unique and creative boards, so be sure your company is creating them.

Matador, an award-winning online travel publication and independent media company, did an amazing job scouting out some of the most creative boards on Pinterest across several industries and topics in early 2012. We're firm believers in the notion that one creative idea always leads to the next, so here are a few of the unique Pinterest boards Matador found. We hope they get your creative wheels turning!

Most home design and interior industry companies opt to show gorgeous living spaces and fabulous homes we can all inspire to live in, so why not take one of your Pinterest boards in a whole other direction? Pinterest user Duncan Moon created an eerie yet beautiful board of visually impactful "Abandoned Places and Things." The photos are well edited, and every single high-quality shot is worth taking a larger-view look at. This is a truly unique approach at showcasing interesting buildings and spaces around the world.

Pinning the opposite of what followers expect to see can make you stand out among your Pinterest peers.

If you have a tech-based company or operate within this industry, chances are your customers and clients would love to be able to look to you to inform them about the latest in technological advances and cool gadgets. An interactive tech board full of photos and videos of some of the most fascinating and exciting advances and products to come would be perfect—and likely attract a lot of attention. Pinterest user Russ Burtner created a compelling Pinterest board called "Envisioning & Technology Trends" to showcase and share some of the amazing technology trends the future has to offer. True tech fans will want to come back to a board like this again and again.

Pinning cutting-edge information for your industry brings followers back to your boards for more of what they like.

For more and more individuals these days, running a blog or free-lance writing for several blogs is a full-time job and their primary career. If your business revolves around blogging, consider taking the Pinterest marketing approach bloggers Heather Shugarman and Julie Grice did. These two savvy women created a collaborative board with "Pins of posts, articles, & information to feed the blogger in you!" Their extensive board shows a real depth of knowledge on the part of these two bloggers, and the curated tips are excellent. We give these two bloggers an A+ for marketing using Pinterest.

Pin articles and information that show you're an expert in your field.

Creative approaches to food have been gaining in popularity among "foodies." If you're in the event-planning or food industry, you're probably all too familiar with new and unusual requests. Why not have some fun with this new fascination for interesting food? Pinterest user Christina Allen's "Hooked on the Brothers" board features all kinds of unique cakes and cupcakes that feature Nintendo characters Mario and Luigi from the famous *Super Mario Brothers* video game. We like her creative direction with this board and its fun and eye-catching content. If you have a business within this industry, appeal to your Pinterest followers by showing your sense of humor.

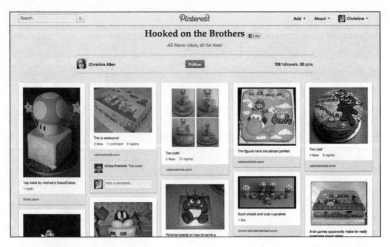

Use humor to create memorable boards and pins.

Last but not least, we want to share one more great tutorial board that can serve a purpose for your brand when it comes to marketing. Throughout your company's development and evolution, you're going to learn a lot as a business owner, or as someone close to the development process. And it's great to be able to pass on knowledge to other aspiring business owners. Not to mention, it's also a great way of becoming a trusted source of information on Pinterest.

If you haven't already, you're going to learn a lot when you start to create stunning images for Pinterest on your website and blog. Why not share the information you find on a website development board? Pinterest user Wendy D created an educational Pinterest board called "Photography Tips" where she shares links to articles and tutorials about taking professional-quality photos. This is a great way for Wendy to share her knowledge and help others. Let Pinterest be a place where you aren't just sharing gorgeous images, but a place where you are sharing useful information, too.

Sharing tips pertinent to your industry or skill is a great way to gain a following.

VERY PINTERESTING!

Most Pinterest users don't see Pinterest for everything it has to offer. Sharing beautiful images is indeed this social media platform's primary function, but there's also a huge opportunity to share helpful information. Pinning informative content makes you a more followed and well-rounded pinner.

Pin Perseverance

As an early adopter, Christine has been on Pinterest since the beginning, and considers herself very fortunate to have been one of the first users on the site. And over the course of the past few years, she's seen brands and various Pinterest users start using the site with a lot of excitement, only to all but completely abandon their accounts. We know several individuals and brands that now regret that decision. But who knew Pinterest was going to become the third most popular social media site on the web?

The moral of the story? It's important to stick with it! Oftentimes, businesses will give up on certain marketing tactics and campaigns before they've given them the proper time and attention to see what the outcome could be. It's always much easier to give up a particular route of marketing and move on to the next, than invest the necessary time and energy to make it successful.

Pinterest is time-consuming, particularly if you want to take the time to source and put forth stellar content. Sure, pinning and repinning takes seconds, but all the work behind the scenes of your Pinterest account can, and most likely will, take time to develop. But with all the incredible traffic statistics being released, and the major increases in revenue many retailers are experiencing due to Pinterest, it would certainly behoove you to stick with it.

One of the best ways to ensure you'll stick with something new is to incorporate it into your schedule right away. While it's on your mind, there's no better time than the present to work Pinterest into your routine. Here are some things to consider when looking through your daily schedule for a place to pencil in Pinterest:

Consider Pinterest's peak hours of usage. Most of the comments, likes, and repins we receive occur in the morning or in the evening, leading us to believe most people like to pin either before or after work. If pinning once a day works for you, choose some time within these peak Pinterest hours.

> **PIN TIP**
>
> Peak social media usage, regardless of the site, is usually around the same time, so if you manage several accounts—for example, both Pinterest and Facebook—try to alternate the time you post or pin to reach people on both platforms at different times. And even if you're sending the same message, tailor it for the site—more visual for Pinterest, more textual for Facebook.

Prep your pins a day in advance. Chances are you're a very busy individual, and sometimes sticking to a schedule doesn't always work. If you have some pins on reserve—perhaps pins you've liked but haven't repinned—you can cover yourself for a day of quick pinning.

Christine likes to prepare for days she knows are going to be busy by spending some free time the day before searching and liking pins she wants to repin. The next day, when she only has about 15 minutes to pin, she repins what she liked the day before.

Many third-party companies are starting to develop around Pinterest, coming up with cool ways to make pinning easier for busy social media people behind brands. Soon enough, there will be ways to be able to time-release pins, much in the same way you can time tweets on Twitter or schedule publications on your blog.

You now have the tools to promote your business on Pinterest. No doubt there will be changes to both Pinterest and your business, but with a plan, some flexibility, perseverance, and creativity, we think you'll find Pinterest a fun and rewarding addition to your marketing efforts.

The Least You Need to Know

- Reflecting minor or regular changes to your company or your inventory on Pinterest can be as easy as creating new boards with the new information.

- Larger changes, like rebranding efforts, may have your company wanting to reach out to a new demographic. Reflect those changes on Pinterest by pinning content to engage your new desired demographic.

- One of the most effective ways to stay present on Pinterest is to continue to think of new and creative ways of marketing on the site. Keep your creative hat on at all times and let the efforts of other pinners inspire you.

- Pinterest is time-consuming, but because of its traffic-driving and marketing capabilities, it's going to be time well spent. The longer you continue to build, the more rewards you will gain.

- Persevering on Pinterest will be much easier if you make it part of your daily routine. If you have limited time to spend on the site, pin and interact during Pinterest's peak hours.

Glossary

agile marketing   The marketing plan style that uses short-term, measurable goals with low-cost programs applied to various media that are expanded if proven successful.

bookmarklet   A button you install on your web browser bookmarks or favorites bar that lets you pin an image directly from a website to your Pinterest profile. Also called *pinmarklet* or *Pin It button*.

brand advocate   An individual who is a fan of a brand to the extent that he feels a sense of ownership over seeing that brand succeed. This volunteer marketer uses his time to promote the brand he loves without receiving payment to do so. Also called *brand ambassador*.

brand narrative   The story of a brand. It comprises the viewpoint, messages, and experiences that tell the past and current history of a brand with consumers.

brand voice   The cohesive and coherent narrative that tells a brand's story throughout all the content the brand puts out.

collaborating   When two or more parties work together toward a common goal and often generate ideas for one another, especially in terms of contributing to pinboards.

contributing   When a pinner sees what's already established on a board and adds to the existing content.

customer profile   A summary that defines the likes, dislikes, personality traits, and characteristics that make up a brand's target customer.

engagement   Refers to any activity between a person and information online. For example, someone who's viewing Pinterest and looking at your pins, boards, or profile is engaged with you via your boards.

false influence   When an influencer repins a noninfluencer's work and the noninfluencer is subsequently flooded with follows, making him appear to have more influence than he really does.

focus group   A group of people who have the characteristics of your ideal customer. Moderators ask for their opinion about your company or products, and you use those opinions to improve your business.

hashtag   A word or phrase preceded by the hash or pound symbol (#). Hashtags make the word or phrase searchable, making it a keyword. Hashtags are mostly used on social media platforms to create conversations or exchanges about a specific topic.

hat tip   The act of virtually tipping your hat to someone who spurred an idea or creation. A movement is in motion to use two attribution symbols: ∽ or the word *via* for direct reference and ⤳ or the words *hat tip* for hat tip.

influencer   A Pinterest user who has a lot of followers who look to her for advice and suggestions. An influencer influences her followers' buying decisions.

keyword   Words associated with your product, service, or company that are used by search engines. Include keywords in your profile, board, and pin descriptions, and you'll appear in Pinterest searches and more likely to appear in web search results, too.

micro-blogging   The posting of very short entries or updates on a blog or social networking site.

mind mapping   A way to visually and conceptually organize and generate ideas to brainstorm in an attempt to solve problems, make decisions, and solidify plans. The key concept or problem is at the center, and ideas extend outward in hub and spoke style, but they can also be connected to each other.

passive advertising A marketing tactic that keeps your name or brand and products or services in front of potential customers. On Pinterest, you accomplish this with your boards and your pins on other pinners' boards. The message isn't "Buy our stuff!" but "Look at what we do!"

permalink A URL that links to a specific story or post, as opposed to linking to the overall website or a single web page. Short for *permanent link*, permalinks allow you to access the original image or the blog, article, instructions, etc. associated with the image.

pin addict A Pinterest user who would consider himself an advocate of the site. This person spends a considerable amount of time using Pinterest.

pin sources An organized collection of bookmarked websites where you can find guaranteed content to pin with ease.

pin stream The continuous stream of pins you can see when you view a profile through **Pins** (pinterest.com/*yourwebsiteURL*/pins). In a pin stream view, pins appear with the most recent up top.

pinboard Another name for board.

pinfluential A pinner who has enough followers on Pinterest that her actions and the content she pins become highly influential to other users.

Pinterest perfect storm brand A brand ideally suited for Pinterest because of the visual content it produces and demographic it targets.

power pinner A Pinterest user with a very large following. A power pinner wields a great deal of internet influence.

search engine optimization (SEO) The process of identifying and using specific words, phrases, and images on your web pages, blogs, and pins that help you appear among the top results of web searches.

search engine status The rank you have in search engines like Google or Yahoo! The higher your rank—that is, the higher on the list you appear when someone searches for keywords that appear on your website—the better your status and the more likely the searcher will visit your website.

sponsored pin   A paid-for pin presented by an influential Pinterest user for a brand in an effort to increase brand awareness and potentially drive traffic and sales for that brand.

vlog   Similar to written blogs, vlogs are video blogs posted and promoted using the same marketing methods as a text blog. They're often posted to YouTube or Vimeo, too, which broadens the audience reach beyond blog subscribers.

waterfall marketing   The marketing plan style that focuses on long-term goals and repeats familiar, strategic, and often costly programs.

Resources

You're probably familiar with and may read the business and financial dailies, weeklies, and monthlies (*Financial Times*, *BusinessWeek*, and *Forbes*, for example) as well as the publications and websites pertinent to your business sector. And that's not to mention the number of enewsletters and blogs to which you can subscribe to stay on top of trends, hot topics, and important happenings. You could spend your entire business day, if not close to all your waking hours, just keeping up. Here are a few others we found useful while writing this book that produce good social media marketing content on a regular basis:

American Express OPEN Forum
openforum.com
Targeted to small business, this site is a good resource for businesses with varied levels of experience in social media.

ClearSaleing
clearsaleing.com
Log on here to download the Online Advertising Study we mention in the book.

eMarketer
emarketer.com
Subscribe to eMarketer's enewsletter for news and tips for online marketing. This site also produces webinars about social media marketing.

Mashable
mashable.com
Log on here for daily tech-related news across various industries and locations.

Search Engine Land
searchengineland.com
This site offers tips and reports on search engine optimization.

SEOmoz
SEOMoz.com
This community site offers some great insight into social media and the SEO implications.

Social Media Examiner
socialmediaexaminer.com
This website keeps you up to date on the latest happenings in social media.

The Social Media Marketing Blog
scottmonty.com
Ford's social media manager, Scott Monty, blogs about his experience and offers advice.

Social Media Today
socialmediatoday.com
This comprehensive social media news site offers articles, reports, and a weekly Best Thinkers Series webinar featuring presentations from top social media strategists.

Zuberance
zuberance.com
Zuberance offers news, studies, and single-topic reports, and hosts events about brand advocacy.

The following people offer workshops and courses on business and marketing planning. You'll find lots of resources on their websites as well:

Marie Forleo, *B-School*
marieforleo.com
Ms. Forleo's B-School conference is a sell-out event. Even if you can't attend, her website offers lots of free advice, and you can sign up for weekly vlogs that rock.

Jennifer Lee, *The Right-Brain Business Plan*
rightbrainbusinessplan.com
Ms. Lee offers online and in-person courses as well as a book for
building your business plan in an innovative and visual way that ties
in beautifully with the Pinterest mind-set. The tactics she presents
can easily translate from your business plan to your marketing plan.

Eric Schwartzman, *Social Media Boot Camp*
ericschwartzman.com/pr/schwartzman/socialmediabootcamp.aspx
Mr. Schwartzman presents his Social Media Boot Camp interna-
tionally and is often asked to speak at conferences regarding social
media. His website offers tools to help you plan your overall
marketing strategy.

Index

C

D

I

L

J-K

M

X-Y-Z